YES TO IT ALL

Stories from the Edges of Love

Genevieve Kim

To request permissions, contact support@genevievekim.com

Published by Genevieve Kim LLC

Visit www.genevievekim.com

These are my memories, from my perspective, and I have tried to represent events as faithfully as possible. Some names in the book have been changed to protect individuals' privacy. This book does not replace the advice of a medical professional. Consult your physician before making any changes to your health plan.

Edited by: Desiree de Lunae
Book design by: Genevieve Kim
Photographs by: Genevieve Kim

ISBN: 979-8-218-05006-1

For my grandmothers,
and yours

"Faith is an oasis in the heart which will never be reached by the caravan of thinking."

- KHALIL GIBRAN

STORIES FROM THE EDGES OF LOVE

Foreward

You are about to meet my wildly creative, intensely opinionated, edgy, stylish, ride-or-die, soul sister friend... Genevieve Kim.

We have two and a half decades of life together. And let me tell you, it is never boring. In this gripping memoir, Genevieve takes you through many adventures of the soul. This life is one grand experiment, and she tests it all out to uncover the treasures of truth that echo through the ages. I have been there in the background to witness these journeys. The years have been filled with hopeless despair, spiritual crises, miraculous soul healings, "only God could do that" moments, satisfying victories and conversations that last till the wee hours of the morning.

Above all, she is an artist. Genevieve wanders this planet in search of stories worth telling. Whether it's through photography, digital media, written word, or coaching the creative in their message and mission, her skill and devotion to self-expression is nothing short of remarkable. She brings into focus the stories that long to be noticed. From stories of forgotten refugees in Lebanon, to a visionary leader in a community, to the homeless man who is often bypassed, to the artist who struggles with depression, Genevieve values that each human is seen and heard. And in this memoir, we are lucky to hear her story: how to love yourself through pain, how to live your dharma, how to trust in self and Spirit, and how to break the molds that the world insists we replicate. She cuts into the core of what matters and unearths the sacred part of our being.

There are many hurdles in being an artist today. A creative entrepreneur will need to navigate treacherous terrains of the ego and of the collective at large. Dealing with crippling doubt, constantly pushing the edges of what's common and normal, and clear expression are but a few challenges to overcome as an artist. But Genevieve tells the tale of the artist, and how it is a journey worth taking.

Despite the objections, criticisms, and abuse she has endured from family, previous partners, peers, the education system, the health system, and corporate America, this free spirit never abandoned her art. She paves her own way and encourages others to do the same. Genevieve's tenacity and stubbornness in honoring herself is to be admired. I have learned from her to be devoted to my craft, to accept my gifts and continue creating.

This memoir will delight your imagination, open your heart to yourself and to humanity, and give you courage to just be you. I love seeing the world through Genevieve's eyes. She enlivens your senses and jolts you out of the humdrum life.

Grab a tea, sit outside, and enjoy a stroll in the cosmos with our dear friend Gen.

Sincerely,
Desiree de Lunae, L.Ac. M.S.T.O.M.

Introduction

Hello friend. Welcome to my first book. Whew~
I wrote this memoir with the intent to share just how beautiful the mess and chaos of life can be. According to my astrological birth chart, the stars aligned such that I'd be born with a difficult family life, the sensitivity and shyness of a crab, the wandering nature of a lone wolf, creative neuroses, and a penchant for beauty. My chart also shows that I am meant to experience life through trial and error. This explains why my CV looks like Frankenstein put it together, and why I leave the "Permanent Mailing Address" field blank.

The fact that I was born on an auspicious day—the 2nd of November, *Dia de Los Muertos* (Day of the Dead) or All Souls' Day—will tell you a lot about me. I was put here to learn about life through death. Can't tell you how many expectations have crumbled before my eyes or how many painful goodbyes I've said.

If "life is like a box of chocolates…you never know what you're gonna get," as Forrest Gump's mother says, then I'd still buy the whole box. (But don't think I don't have my preferences—definitely dark chocolate toffee over the nasty cherry truffles.) The scavenge would still be worth the mess.

Over time, I learned that the most challenging chapters I lived through had the greatest lessons for me to learn. Nothing in my life was random at all. In fact, I was born to live this very life—not someone else's or some other way, but this one. It's rather non-linear, with a great deal of "GPS recalculating" moments—in large part because of my curious nature and because I can't help but stray down a rabbit hole.

My understanding of why and how I got here will no doubt evolve, but I'd like to take a moment at this juncture in my life, to reflect on what makes me wake up each morning and not let my nihilistic side take over.

If your GPS is recalculating, you're in good company. We can hang out here together for a few pages or so. This memoir is a kaleidoscope of some of the fractals that have helped me embrace a life lived without a map.

With love~
Genevieve Kim
Sintra, Portugal
20 April 2022

1

MAGIC CARPET RIDE

17 July, 2016. Memories while in Cappadocia, Turkey

Magic Carpet, can you find her for me?

We float through space and time. There I am at 23; she's sitting in the basement of Georgetown's Blommer Library. I watch her from the window as she closes her book and runs out of the building.

"I can't do it anymore, Des. I'm losing it. I can't breathe. I can't think—"

"You *do* know what to do," Desiree says on the other end of the phone.

She goes back into the library and packs up all her belongings. There will be no more studying.

Magic Carpet, where is she going? I don't think she's okay. We should fol-

low her to be sure.

She runs to catch up with a few of her post-bacc classmates for a round of drinks. "Finally, you're coming out with us for drinks! Where have you been all semester?" She doesn't answer. Her mind is elsewhere. When they walk into the bar off Q St., she heads straight to the bartender and orders a shot of tequila. Then another. And on her third, she yells, "I have to head home now, but I'll be out more. No more of this B.S. controlling. I'm done. I'm going home. It's over!" After dropping $20 on the table, she heads out.

Magic Carpet, follow her until she gets home.

***

"Don't ask me why I'm home late or where I've been. I'm done. It's over. I'm leaving."

"Not this shit again."

"No. I can't do this anymore."

"This is so typical of you. I have a big meeting tomorrow. You're trying to get me fired, aren't you? You know what they'd call you in the army? A blue-falcon. You know what that stands for? Buddy-fucker. That's what you are."

Midway through his lecture, she says, "What if I told you I cheated on you?" Though still a little fiery from the tequila, she knew it was not the alcohol talking. The tequila had merely rehydrated the shriveled raisin she had become. Tired of his mind games, she decided it was her turn to do the mind-fucking. She knew what his Achilles heel was. Why else had he hacked into her emails, opened her text messages, read through her diary, and questioned every guy he saw mentioned? Like a bee with only one stinger, she attacked knowing this would be the beginning of the end. The ultimate sabotage.

"You're lying. You're just saying that. Did you?"

"If I said yes, would you still make me stay?"

"Damnit! Just say whether you did or not?" She could see that he had been stung.

A few days prior, he had told her they would not be going to San Diego for the holidays. Instead, he had booked a diving trip in St. Lucia for Christmas. "We just did Thanksgiving with your family. You promised we would alternate holidays with each of our families and said we'd spend Christmas with my family. Why did you book a trip without asking me?"

"I didn't want to be the one to tell you this, but I don't think it will be healthy for you to see your family. It's for your own good."

"What do you mean?"

"Your family doesn't love you. Especially your sister. I can tell by the way she talks to you that she doesn't care about you. She's jealous of you. You're just too naive to see it. Can't you see I'm protecting you?"

"How dare you talk about my sister like that. She's been there for me my whole life."

"Your voice is getting loud again. Clearly, you're getting emotional. Until you've calmed down, we're not going to discuss this further."

[8]

He may have been able to convince her that his family thought poorly of her, or that her friends and co-workers didn't like her, but she would not allow him to make her doubt her family. As sideways as her family's love looked, she knew deep down that they cared.

It was a mistake to have walked down the aisle, but she would not make the mistake of living a lie under the control of someone else's insecurities and wounds. Under the confines of what a Korean father-in-law expected of her; what the wife of an ex-military officer ought to look like; or how the daughter-in-law of an heir should behave. No amount of stability and comfort in the known would be able to keep her handcuffed in a relationship that kept her restrained from free thought, from free expression, from being able to live her own story.

She went to bed that night knowing that she had unraveled that which could not be rewound. For the first time in their relationship, she had no doubts. She would stand by her decision to leave, no matter the consequences.

That night, relief turned into a deep slumber. She had resolved to sleep on the couch, alone, knowing that this would be her life for some time.

Magic Carpet, not so close!

The woman on the couch suddenly opens her eyes. Was it paranoia to think that perhaps he had come out with his gun? Her body freezes to play possum.

Magic Carpet, do you think she saw us? Did you see how she woke up in a panic?

[9]

After some time, her body began to relax. No, she would not play possum to the fears. She would face them. At that moment, a lightness overcame her, bringing a deep assurance that everything would be all right. Even if it meant ending up homeless without a cent to her name, she knew she had to leave. Jump and see where you will fly. Her back expanded. The rope that had bound her so tightly to him unraveled, and out the wings came.

Magic Carpet, thank you for bringing me back here. It's a blessing to be reminded of my journey and to know that it was you I felt there in the room that night.

Goodnight, Genevieve. Everything's going to be okay.

Nevşehir, Turkey, 2016

2

I HEAR YOU

The San Diego Opera audition would be my first after the divorce. Less than a year prior, just seven months into my marriage, I found myself packing as quickly as possible so I could leave my ex-husband while he was at work. There were many red flags before getting married, but I stayed until the relationship crushed nearly all the spirit out of me. During our three years together, I experimented with self-destructive behaviors, including cutting and hitting myself, and I had my first major depressive episode. One morning, while looking in the mirror, I couldn't recognize the ghost that stood before me. I had to get out.

Nine months later, I received an invitation to audition with the San Diego Opera. It took me by surprise, given the audition demo I submitted was subpar by my standards. My confidence hung by a thread after the divorce, yet I felt a tinge of hope that perhaps this audition would lead to the fresh start I needed. Halfway through my audition, however, the director stopped me and, without explanation, asked me to leave. In less than a song, my hopes of performing on stage evaporated.

I blamed myself for the disaster of an audition. "If only I had never met my husband, I would not have lost my focus on music." As I left the audition, I resolved never to sing again.

I spent the next several years of my life getting a "real" career. I graduated from Duke University's Fuqua School of Business with an M.B.A. concentration in finance. Before graduating, I had already secured a job at one of the most competitive management consulting firms. On paper, my life looked put together, but underneath the gold veneer, my self-destructive behaviors worsened. Eating disorders, drugs, and more toxic relationships suffocated me. Cycles of anxiety and depressive episodes intensified. Apathy sucked me dry and left me wondering whether I should keep living or not. I had become all but mute.

During my second year of grad school, the school psychologist asked me, "Is there anything you do enjoy?"

"Photography," I said.

"Then just photograph," he said.

"Just photograph?"

"Yep. Just photograph."

That was all the permission I needed to loosen my grip on self-punishment.

***

The following term, I headed to Italy for a semester study exchange. When I got there, my camera and I became inseparable. We savored more than pasta and wine; together, we soaked up as much design, literature, art, music, beauty, history, and architecture as possible. On one of our long walks around the city, my camera led me to a side of town I had not yet explored. Across the street, I noticed a photogenic building and curiously walked toward it. We were in front of La Scala Opera House.

Though I had no intention of becoming a professional musician, something told me to start singing again. That evening, I messaged an old friend who used to study voice in Italy and asked if she knew of any teachers in Milan. She responded "yes" and connected me with a teacher of hers. A few weeks later, I started taking voice lessons.

After our first lesson, my voice coach asked, "Why did you ever stop singing? You have a beautiful voice."

"I suppose it was my way of punishing myself, but I'm done with that now."

***

Upon returning to the States, I signed up for my grad school's annual talent show. This was my first time on stage since that disastrous audition seven years prior. My voice roared throughout the auditorium. Even when the music ended, I kept singing. The audience went wild. Standing ovation. My punishment was over.

They heard me. *I* heard me.

I have a voice, and I'm going to learn how to use it again, no matter how long it takes.

Teatro alla Scala, Milan, Italy, 2014

3

DEAR STACY

Dear Stacy,

I'm not sure if you remember me, but I've never forgotten you.

When you fired me from the Kohl's project, my world shook a seismic 9.0. I vividly remember the walk to meet you in the Kohl's building, through aisles of cubicles underneath fluorescent lighting and asbestos-looking ceilings. I opened one of the conference rooms to find you seated next to the window with a view of the bleak parking lot, filled with hundreds of employee cars.

When I received the calendar invite to meet with you one-on-one, I knew it wasn't a social call. I discovered from others on the team that I had been excluded from the email threads regarding the upcoming client presentation. Earlier in the week, Kevin reviewed my deliverables and asked me, "Do you even know what this project is about?" I had been on the project for three months, and evidently, I was clueless. Even the younger analysts on the team were flying faster than me.

You brought me on to some of the best projects, and for that, I am grateful. But more than that, I want to thank you for being so honest with me, something I could not be for myself. You asked me a single question: "Do you want to be here?" I tried to muster up, "Of course, I want to be here," but I could not. As I struggled to hold my tears, it was evident that I did not want to be there.

Stormy Seas, Batroun, Lebanon, 2016

During team meetings, I was distracted by thoughts of ending it all. When I'd get back to my hotel room, I would try to catch up on what I had not been able to do at the office, but I struggled to focus on the work ahead of me. The tension worsened with each passing day. Thoughts of worthlessness haunted me every waking moment, from the phrasing of a single slide title to the graphics I chose for client presentations. *No, not that one, dumbass. Delete. Do it again.* Every click of the mouse confirmed just how much of an imposter I was.

Only the smartest and most talented worked on strategy projects, from which I had been let go. Confidence shattered, I no longer knew what I brought to the table. After leaving your project, I moved to operations. I staffed myself on the most tedious and mundane project possible, working on anti-money laundering. *Whoopie.* The upside was that this project did not require me to get on a plane every week, and I could work from the 47th floor of Rockefeller Center, a much better view than the one back at Kohl's.

Instead of ending the day in a sterile hotel room, I came home to my apartment and cried myself to sleep in my own bed. That lasted for only a few months until I would walk out of a client meeting sweating with pain in my chest and stomach. I called my sister-in-law, a doctor, to tell her my symptoms. I asked, "Am I having a heart attack? My neck is tingling, and my chest is tight." She said likely not but to get checked out to be sure.

I went to the hospital and was diagnosed with a stomach ulcer and a panic attack. Even my body knew the answer to your question before I did. Clearly, I did not want to be there. After discharging myself from the hospital, I decided to quit.

Two weeks later, I emailed my resignation letter. No safety net. No backup job. No plan. I had to triage myself back to life.

For months I had tried scheduling an appointment to see a therapist, but with the unpredictable hours at the office, I had to cancel sessions. After quitting, though, I finally got professional help. I learned that I had severe depression and confessed for the first time that I had been looping in suicidal ideation, something I had been too ashamed to admit.

Not everything about working in consulting sucked, though. In every project evaluation, managers would tell me that I needed to improve my storytelling skills, which happened to be the one skill I wanted to improve. It didn't matter how fast I could create pivot tables in Excel or whether I could work with large data sets. I fell in love with making beautiful presentations, which would be my introduction to information and graphic design.

I left consulting about four months after you let me go from the Kohl's project, and I have to say, if it weren't for your honesty, I wouldn't have hit rock bottom and discovered what I wanted more than anything else in the world. All I wanted to do was travel the world, tell stories and connect with the human spirit. I wanted to be working with communities, not big box retailers.

Because of you, my life took a huge turn. About a year after leaving management consulting, I found myself on the other side of the world photographing for UN Habitats in Lebanon. Shortly after, I started a photography project that traveled to 16 countries, across five continents. Though I had never sold a photo print before, leaping into photography seemed less foolish than staying in a job that was literally eating at my insides.

Getting fired was not a failure, but a gift that pushed me in the right direction. If you had not kicked me off the project, I don't know if I would have been able to leave consulting on my own. What I feared most was the unknown of failing, but the real failure was not listening to my heart's yearning.

Several years after leaving consulting, I sent a photo print to one of the partners who had mentored me. She had been the one to recruit me and had been such an extraordinary believer in my abilities. She was also the one who had helped me exit this chapter of my life with as much ease and grace as possible. It felt as if I had come full circle in gifting her the print.

Along the way, I've come to embrace my ennui of small talk at team dinners. This starfish no longer cuts off her arms to fit in a box. I'm more than comfortable with the fact that I don't give a damn about making presentations for those focused solely on the bottom line, and I refuse to do work that drains my values. Thank god, because I love what I do today-- filling the world with beautiful stories. Each of us is a unique piece in a grander mosaic, and our edges have a specific place and purpose.

Though I don't reckon you remember who I am, I remember who you are. In my story, you will go down as the earthquake that shook me to my core. You helped me close a chapter and begin writing the next. Thank you.

Genevieve Kim

Photo I gifted to partner at the firm, Cappadocia, Turkey, 2016

4

TRIPOD AND TIMER

You know how everyone expects Asians to be stellar at math? Well, I am probably the single statistical error of this stereotype. Take, for example, this math problem:

Farmer Hannah has 25 sheep and 23 goats on the farm. Last night some of her sheep escaped. If she still has 9 sheep in the pen, how many sheep escaped?

You might think this is a simple subtraction problem, but it wasn't so straightforward to me. I began wondering if something else had happened to the sheep. Maybe a jealous neighbor stole them in the middle of the night. Or perhaps a pack of wolves ate them. What about the goats? Maybe they had something to do with their disappearance. What all of these scenarios, I could not be certain how many had *escaped*. When I asked my parents to help me with my math homework, I got an earful about how disappointing it was that I couldn't do simple arithmetic. I learned early on that asking for help would only get me into trouble. Better not to ask for help.

No surprise that when it came time to learn photography, I kept to myself. I read books, watched YouTube videos, and learned through trial and error, all in place of taking photography classes.

I practiced photographing on my morning solo walks. Occasionally, I'd spot another street photographer. You can always spot the street photographers—it's in the quiet way they blend into the environment and observe the scenes around them with a camera at their side.

On one of my walks, a street photographer approached me and asked, "What are you photographing?"

"Benches," I said. So much happened on New York's benches. Lovebirds, nappers, readers, dealers, dog owners, loud cellphone talkers, smokers—all wrapped up in their island on a bench.

"What about you?" I asked.

"Street fashion," he said. "I noticed your style and wanted to ask if I could photograph you."

"Me?" I asked. My place was behind the camera, not in front.

"Yeah. Stand over here," he directed. I felt awkward and sorry for wasting his time. But after a few frames, he proudly showed me some of the photos.

"Nice! Where do you post these?"

"On Instagram. Here. Check out some of the others I've done."

As I looked through his grid, I was amazed by the colors of the images. "What camera are you using?"

"I switched to the Fuji. The colors are incredible," he said.

We then nerded out on camera gear for an hour or so. I learned so much that afternoon.

Over time, my connection with the New York street photography community expanded. There was Jean-Andre, who took polaroid street portraits on the east side of Prince and Broadway. Unlike digital photography, with polaroids, you can't just spray and pray, especially with the rare kind of film Jean-Andre was using. It costs nearly $3 per click. You have to understand timing and lighting. To this day, Jean-Andre's portrait of me is still my favorite. We became street photography friends, always saying hello whenever we saw each other, and we'd talk about the projects we wanted to do next. I loved our conversations.

Another friend I made while photographing on the streets was an art vintage bookseller on the other side of Prince and Broadway. Frank had a rare collection of artist monographs, many of which included photographers. One morning he called after me, "Hey Genevieve, I got a book I think you'll like." It was a compilation of female Magnum photographers. I had admired the Magnum cooperative for their work in photojournalism, especially Henry Cartier-Bresson and Robert Capa, whom I studied dearly. The founders of Magnum had all been men, so when I saw a book dedicated to the women of Magnum, I took the book home to study every page and see what other stories could be told that weren't just the ones men found interesting.

It became one of the most important photography books for me. I discovered Eve Arnold, whose life and work inspired me on every level. Here was a woman, unafraid to travel to some of the most remote places in the world in the 1950s and '60s. She didn't photograph war. Instead, she made images of rural China, Inner Mongolia, and beyond. If she could do it then, I could do it now.

While I had opened myself up to asking others questions about photography, I was still shy about working alongside one. But that would change the week before I left New York.

As I was selling all my things and moving out of my apartment in New York, I got an unexpected message on Instagram. It was from a friend I had met nearly a decade prior in Seoul, Korea. We had been in the same summer program at Seoul National University. Two Korean-Americans, going back to their roots.

He had just moved back to New York to be with his frail grandmother after spending months on the road filming, and he came across my account and discovered that I was in New York photographing. Within a few days of that first message, we met up at Vanessa's Dumplings on the Lower East Side.

"It's insane that we're crossing paths again after all these years."

"I know. You look good."

"And you look so different." His long, thick black hair accentuated the new edges of his face, no longer carrying the round cheeks of the sophomore I remembered. "Long hair looks good on you."

"Yeah, I've intentionally stopped cutting it. Think about how our Korean ancestors all had long hair. We lost all that with acculturation." For centuries, Korean tradition forbade men and women to cut their hair, as hair was considered a sacred legacy from their parents. But when the Japanese colonized Korea, the *sangtu*, the bun that signified the rite of passage of boys becoming men, was decapitated, thereby, emasculating an entire population. This practice began with the castration of King Gojung's *sangtu*, and continued down to the young boys in school. On the other side of the Pacific Ocean, during the same time, hair politics was also in full force in the U.S. The government withheld rations from indigenous men who did not cut their hair.

My friend's documentary projects were about the preservation and remembrance of culture. He had been working on a documentary film of his 98-year-old grandmother, who had survived bullet wounds from the Korean War. Nothing and everything had changed since we had last seen each other. We were still Korean Americans traveling between cultures, yet we had both changed our names in our time apart. He now went by his Korean name, Myeong, instead of his easy-to-pronounce American name, Shawn, and I was now Genevieve Kim, no longer a Mrs.

"So, how much longer are you here for?"

"I'm leaving next week, flying to San Diego to see my parents for the holidays, and then I'm going to travel to Turkey, Lebanon, and Greece. That's the plan for now. Things may change. Now that I've left my job, there's no reason for me to stay in New York. I've sold almost everything except my bed and a few things."

"Your apartment is empty?"

"Pretty much." As I said that, I read the flash going through his

[26]

mind. "Wait, what if we used my place as a studio? We can do some photos before I go."

"Let's do it. I'll go back and get my gear."

"Now?"

"Yeah. I'll be back. Give me your address."

I rushed to my place to clean up some of the remaining clutter in my apartment. No sooner had I finished when the buzzer rang.

"Come up to the fourth floor."

He walked in with a backpack full of gear. We nerded out on gear for a bit.

"What do you use the 24mm for?"

"It's great when you're in tighter spaces." His whole system was different than mine. He had a full-frame Canon Mark II, whereas I had the crop Canon 70D. I had been eyeing the Mark but wasn't sure if I was ready for the upgrade. Did I want to invest another several thousand dollars into photography? Even though I had already quit a six-figure job to pursue photography, there was still a part of me that wasn't sure if I was ready for the "professional" level camera.

"Do you have any lights?"

"Yeah, this halogen desk lamp."

"That'll work. What about some tape?"

"I got plenty of packing tape."

"Cool. Do you have a timer?"

"Yep. I've never used it, so you'll have to show me how."

"It's awesome to have for self-portraits. Where's your tripod?"

"Here." I had barely touched it since purchasing it.

Myeong started turning my apartment into a makeshift studio. He taped my small desk lamp to his tripod with the packing tape.

"Where are we going to shoot?"

"Here," he said, pointing to the bed.

Then he mounted his camera atop my tripod.

"Are you going to use your 24mm?"

"Yep."

I was surprised by how close he placed the tripod to the bed. Had we used my camera and lens, we would not have been able to get everything. I looked through the viewfinder of his camera. *Voila*. The bed fit in the frame.

As Frank Ocean played in the background, he continued adjusting the frame, and I began rolling a joint. Teamwork makes the dream work.

Myeong sat at the edge of my bed and took a puff. "Stay there. Just keep breathing." I grabbed my camera and began photographing him. *Click.* "Look over here." *Click.* "Keep going." *Click.* I took a peek at the photos and was amazed by the single light.

"Now it's your turn." He got up and told me he wanted to photograph me.

"I've never been in front of the camera before. You're going to have to direct me."

I was the heaviest I had ever been and felt more unattractive than I had in years. Damn, I didn't want to be scrutinized in front of a camera, but I also didn't want to mess up the flow. *Puff. Here we go.*

Myeong, Lower East Side, New York, 2015

We continued photographing each other over the next several days, up until my last day in New York. I followed his directions and let him guide me in front of the camera, completely raw and naked. The chrysalis that had wrapped me for years in body dysmorphia and eating disorders started dismantling. Nowhere to hide. The camera never lies.

That night was a first for me on so many levels. First time being in front of the camera fully exposed; working side-by-side with a fellow photographer; using my tripod and timer; working with artificial lighting; photographing someone so intimately.

***

A few hours after our last photo session, I closed the door on my Lower East Side apartment for the last time and flew to San Diego. A few months prior, when I told my parents that I had quit my job, they didn't say much. I appreciated their silence, but I knew there'd be a thorough cross-examination regarding my plans when I came home. Sure enough, when I arrived, my father asked me, "So what are you going to do now?"

"Travel and photograph. I'm going to take a road trip to New Mexico, and after that, I'll go to Turkey and Lebanon."

As I waited for the other shoe to drop, my father said, "Be careful out there." I had prepared all my armor for this conversation, but there was no need for it.

The next morning, a loud knock startled me in between dreams. "Come in," I said barely awake.

"You'll need this," my father said as he handed me his tripod. Before

I could say thank you, he walked out of my room.

My father may not have been the one to teach me how to drive or drop me off at college—that was my brother—but he was the one who had shown me how to load a camera with film and take pictures. My father was the one who took me to get my film developed and looked at my photos with me.

As I stared at the tripod, I saw all the treasures my father taught me, including my greatest loves in life—photography, singing, travel, and writing. The same father whom I had resented for so long had been the one who had encouraged me to keep a daily journal from an early age, the one who nagged me to take the karaoke mic with him and organized all our family trips. With the tripod, he had given me his blessing. The little girl in me smiled.

***

After a few months with my family, I began the first leg of my trip, off to Death Valley, California. The silence of the winter desert called me. February 2016, I sped along CA-127 N, a one-lane highway that stretched for miles into a horizon of hills. Hardly any cars were on the road this time of year. Wanting to remember this trip forever, I pulled my car over to the side. I counted to see how many cars would pass by. Only one drove by in five minutes. That would be just enough time. Now adept with the tripod and timer, I set up my gear and made several test shots on the side of the road. Ready to go, I waited for the next car to drive by before setting my tripod in the middle of the highway. In broad daylight, on a highway, where folks drove a minimum of 80 MPH, I made my first self-portrait.

Self-Portrait, Death Valley, California, U.S.A., 2016

I would not have made that photo without Myeong. During our time together in my apartment, I had learned so much, most importantly how to let go and allow myself to be seen. My fears of what I would find on the other side of the camera softened. In the middle of the road, I stood still, knowing that nothing could run me over.

A few hours later, I arrived at the foot of Death Valley's dunes. As I parked my car, I noticed there were only three other cars in the lot. The odds of crossing paths with anyone else out on the dunes were slim. Time to bring my tripod again.

The contours of the dunes beckoned me inside. I walked for some time until I found a perfect crease between the crest of two dunes.

I set up my tripod, mounted my camera, and began undressing—the same way I had back in the apartment.

Cruella de Vil, who holds the award for Nastiest Voice in My Head, began picking at my back fat, and tummy.

"These photos are going to be disgusting. You said you wanted to become a photographer to show beauty, and instead, you're photographing this?"

"Cruella, I'm happy to have you as a passenger on this road trip, but don't be a backseat driver. I'm driving."

In the silence of the dunes, I did my yoga practice as the timer clicked. A review of the photos made me smile.

I look better without my clothes.

That's how my annual ritual of self-portraiture began.

***

Several years later, Myeong visited me while I lived in Lebanon. We went on an excursion a few hours outside of Beirut and hiked up a hill where we came across a cave. Both of us could sense that there were spirits inside, so we decided to say a few prayers out of respect for what we were about to do.

We stopped right outside the mouth of the cave. Myeong thought this would be a good place to take some photos of me. I undressed, crouched on top of one of the boulders, and began slithering in front of the camera. Click. Click. Click.

"Whoa. Where did that come from? When did you learn how to do that?"

"I've been spending more time with the tripod and self-timer."

***

New math problem

If there are two photographers with one tripod and one timer, how many photos can they make?

Self-Portrait, Cappadocia, Turkey, 2016

5

APPLES FALLING
FROM THE TREE

As I steadily approach 42, the age my mother birthed me, I wonder who she would have been had she been born a child of the '70s, like my sisters, or of the '80s like me. Enduring 55 years of marriage with my father, I wonder who she would have been if not a wife or mother.

I asked her if she ever had a dream. Silence. Had I asked a privileged, U.S.-born millennial question? The world my mother grew up in included apartheid under Japanese colonization, World War II, the Korean War, and political instability in a new country called "South Korea." Though my grandmother gave birth to seven children, my mother was the fourth of five surviving children. Two of her brothers had died before the age of two. Child mortality in Korea rose between World War II and the Korean War. For this generation, survival was the dream. Life was black or white—dead or alive.

Seeing that there were no sons in the family, the elders selected my mother to get an education. School was a privilege prioritized for sons. Yet, the elders recognized my mother's intelligence and brazen ways as fit enough to fill a son's shoes. Since there were no schools in her village, she had to move to another city to study; by 13, she was already living on her own. My mother became the first and only of five daughters to attend high school.

The elders had chosen right. My mother went on to graduate from university, which in 1960s South Korea was rare for women to do. Several years later, my mother met my father and got married. Early in her marriage, my mother went to her parents asking for permission to come home. It was unthinkable for a woman of her generation and culture to utter the shameful D word aloud, no less to her pious parents. When she did, her parents turned her away and told her to return to her husband. Divorce was not an option.

Things grew even more challenging for my mother when my father decided to move the family to America. Japan had been the farthest anyone in her family had traveled. She made the leap across the entire Pacific Ocean and immigrated to the U.S. in the early 1970s, when people thought everyone with slanted eyes came from China, before Gangnam Style, K-beauty, and *Squid Games*. She arrived not knowing any English and had no friends or family to confide in when my father took his anger out on her. It was a lonely time for my mother, but with three kids to think about, their survival came first.

A generation later, her daughters would experience their own challenges with marriage. Coincidentally (or fate?), my sisters and I all became brides at the age of 23, with grooms who were 27. Like our mother, we got married not long after graduating university, but marriage is where the divergence of mother-daughter paths would begin and end.

The first daughter

After 15 years of marriage, my oldest sister announced that she and my brother-in-law were getting divorced. We're not entirely shocked by their decision to separate, but we never thought our sister would get a divorce. My oldest sister is a devout Catholic. She attended daily mass and was heavily involved in church community activities. For those who don't know, the Catholic Church's divorce policy is why the King of England chopped off his wives' heads and started his own religion. You're basically an outcast if you get divorced. The Catholic Church has an ex-communication policy banning the divorced from participating in some of the Church's sacraments. Pretty old school, I know, but there are many, including my sister and parents, who do not take the Church's stance lightly.

Throughout their marriage, I never really heard her talk about having a career. Instead, she followed her husband around the country, moving from one professorship to the next. And when my brother-in-law decided to leave the tenure track to start his own venture, it became clear how different their paths were.

After her divorce, she went back to school to get a second bachelor's degree to become a nurse in her 30s, only to discover months later that nunhood was her true calling. (A divorcee as a nun? Yeah, even the Church has loopholes for that, but let's not get sidetracked.) For several years she went through a discernment process to choose which order of nuns she would take her vows with, and when she finally came to a decision, we were definitely shocked. She chose to join a cloistered order. That's the kind of order where once you're in, you're in. No coming out.

The vows of her chosen order included complete renunciation of the material world, including possessions, relationships, and technology. That meant there would be no more phone calls, texts, or casual hellos with my sister. Though she could have visitors several times a year, no physical contact was allowed, and we separated behind an iron grid. My siblings and I joke, "Guess it's that time of year to visit our sister behind bars."

Joking aside, the hardest part was knowing she would not be around for family traditions. Every New Year, all the women in our family gathered around the kitchen table to make Korean dumplings and catch up on life. New Year is one of the few times when we're all in the same city, in the same room. Now, our circle would be incomplete without her. I've never lost a close family member, but I mourned in my sister's absence.

The second daughter

My second older sister started out with dreams of becoming a fashion designer, but chose to get practical and got a Master's in Psychology. She grew a successful marriage-family therapy practice and lived the ultimate suburban dream with her husband, daughter, three-month long travels around the world, big house, boats, cars, motorcycles, etc. But that would change nearly overnight when she and her husband made the decision to sell all their things, stop Jonesing around, and live off-grid in Costa Rica. That was the beginning of the end.

Today, my sister is no longer with her husband and cannot see her own children. The betrayal and heartache my sister has endured would crush just about anyone. Despite the unjust cruelty of the corrupt Costa Rican judicial system, my sister continued living there to serve the less fortunate in her community. Whenever I am in a state of darkness, I remind myself that if my sister, who had her children torn from her arms, could still find light, I could and would, too.

* The third daughter *

I may have been the last to marry but the quickest to divorce. After only seven months of marriage, I knew I would commit some kind of crime if I stayed. If Freud needed a case study on father-daughter and mother-son dynamics, my marriage would be classic textbook. The dynamic between my ex-husband and I mirrored the unresolved issues we had with our mother and father, respectively. Together, we were a deadly cocktail of explosive fighting, ultimatums, and abuse.

Divorce is probably my deepest scar, but if I had to do it all over again, I would. Do you believe in fate or free will? My marriage showed me both. After I got divorced, I spent a great deal of time taking a hard look at myself. *Why had I ignored the signs? Why did I think it was okay for someone who loved me to treat me so poorly? How could I have been so stupid? Why? Why? Why?* For a while, I blamed my parents. But blaming them meant that I, a victim of their parenting and marriage, had nothing to change. After years of going to therapy, reanalyzing, and dissecting every childhood memory, I got tired of asking *Why?* All the who-did-what talk had not helped me find peace. Instead, I had become an addict of resentment and anger. (If you haven't already, you'll learn what that looks like in the *#youtoo?* chapter.)

Marriage, divorce, my parents, and so on, may have been part of my karmic destiny, whether I liked it or not, but I had the choice to either continue living out the cycles of intergenerational trauma or learn how to live with compassion—beginning with myself.

***

For years, my mother would blame each of her daughters for having failed in their marriages. "I told you you should never have married him," or "Why couldn't you have just been more patient? You should have stuck it out." But when my father asks me if I ever plan to get remarried, my mother responds with, "She's better off not getting married again. What's the point? Don't get married. Stay single," all right in front of her husband. My mother has never been one for subtlety. She speaks her truth as bluntly as she tenderizes a thick piece of steak. But the truth she skirted since the day her parents turned her away is one that her daughters would eventually know: *You don't have to be a martyr in your marriage.*

Perhaps my mother's marriage was karmic destiny. As apples don't fall far from the tree, the fruit my mother bore were daughters who learned to ripen in winter and spring.

Winter; Santa Fe; New Mexico; 2016

6

#YOUTOO?

I grew up not knowing what it meant to be a woman except that it kind of sucked. Let's start with the toys. *Barbie?* Are you shitting me? I hated dolls, but as a girl, I got them every Christmas and birthday. I wanted Legos, paints, and water guns, not some plastic doll with nasty tangly hair and a boyfriend who looked nothing like the kind of boy I'd want to kiss.

It sounds like I'm picking on Barbie and Ken, so let me be fair. I hated *all* dolls. They creeped me out in a Chuckie kind of way, especially the ones that could open and close their eyes. Once, one of my presents opened its eyes while sitting in a corner. I started screaming and crying. My mother came running in wondering what had happened, but when she saw the doll, she immediately got rid of it.

When I got to middle school, I discovered that being a girl was bloody hell. In seventh grade, I went to the bathroom only to discover that I had a huge stain of blood on my shorts. No. NO. *NO!* I had just walked around the school with a big blot of blood on my ass. I quickly took my sweater off, and wrapped it around my waist, hoping no one saw anything. But all I could feel was an absolute embarrassment. When I got back to class, I noticed that my seat was smeared as well.

After my first period, I bled every two to three weeks. I had no understanding of what my pubescent body was doing. Some mornings I'd wake up with stained sheets, and my mother would scold me for not being more careful, but how was I to know when my hormones would spike?

I wondered what I had to look forward to as a grown woman. But when I looked at my mother and the other Korean women I knew, what I discovered was glum.

• In Korean culture, your gender means everything. Paternal relatives are addressed with the prefix *jin*, which translates to "real"; maternal ones are addressed with the prefix *oe*, which translates to "outsider." The word "foreigner" in Korean also uses the root *oe*. So essentially, your mother's side of the family is an "outsider." Fitting for someone who is just there to breed, right?

• What I also learned is that women are life-long servants. Men don't have to cook or clean up after themselves. That's what a mom, wife, or daughter is for. When my nephew was helping me make gravy one Thanksgiving, my father told his grandson, "You're not supposed to be in the kitchen. Don't you have something better to do?" And even when my mother had one of her terrible migraines, my dad would still ask for his home-cooked meal.

• Not only are you a servant to your husband, but also to your mother-in-law. No matter how hard you tried to keep up with the household or buy her favorite fruits, you could never please her. A mother-in-law's cruelty to a daughter-in-law knew no boundaries: "It's no wonder if you can't make a proper kook, soup, that you can't bare a son." Korean mothers-in-law perpetuated the cycle of misogyny with demands for a grandson. My grandmother had not received the memo that the sperm that completes the chromosomal pairing, XX or XY. It was only on my mother's third child that she had fulfilled her duties as a wife-- the first two, you ask? They were just girls.

• Even up until the day you die, women mean nothing. When I visited our grandparents' tomb, I asked my mother about the names on the gravestones. It was a listing of the family lineage. I saw my brother's name but didn't see my sisters'. That's odd, I thought. But then my mother explained that only the men were listed. Every man comes from a woman. Is that not noteworthy?

• Double standards made it more clear that it was better to be a boy. My older brother got to come and go as he pleased, but I had to be home by 10 p.m. or else. My sisters and I were forbidden to have boyfriends, but my brother had girlfriends.

One of them even got to stay the night. But when my fiancée came to see my family, he wasn't allowed to sleep in the house. "How come Obba (older brother in Korean) gets to stay out late?" The whole debate would come to an end with, "Because he's a boy."

Then there's the Catholic upbringing that reminded me every Sunday that God is a man and that women can't be gods, angels, or disciples. Instead, women could only be prostitutes or surrogates. The angel didn't give Mary much of an option when he gave her the news that she was pregnant. If women did have power, they were either mad Jezebels or cunning Salomes who destroyed men. And we all know what happened to Eve. She took on all the blame for what the snake, the one that God created, had tricked her into eating. I'm not sure what the moral here is: that women are easily fooled or that they deserve to suffer.

I had another thought in mind. Women were weak. Yes. *Weak.* I could not understand how and why my mother remained in an abusive marriage for so many years. Why didn't she leave for fuck's sake—no, for her children's sake? When the #metoo movement exploded across the media, rage took over me. "You cowards. You played dumb Barbie and kept your mouth shut instead of walking out when you knew something was wrong. It's all your goddamn fault we're in this mess. Your silence was compliance. Why didn't you leave? Mom, why? Maybe if you spoke up sooner, we wouldn't be in all this pain.

"Now you're just whining. You're saying #metoo, but you didn't do anything until it was too late, and hundreds of other women fell victim to the same assholes." If all the women in Iceland could go on strike, why couldn't the women of Hollywood, who had so much more of a platform, do the same? Why did it take them so long to speak out? They waited until a red carpet event to dress up in black and say #metoo, whereas when I left seven months into my marriage, it wasn't some publicity stunt. No. I got out because I didn't want there to be another #metoo."

That's when my unconscious whispered *If you can't beat them, join them.* And join them I did. I joined the bro club. I vowed never to allow myself to be vulnerable so that no man could ever control me again. For years, I studied men and became one of them. I ended up graduating from the same MBA program that had denied my ex-husband admission. I kept silent when my brother questioned my ability to go to business school or told me not to get my hopes up by applying to such-and-such school. I ignored him and graduated from one of the top business schools and got a higher-paying job than he'd ever had. No man would ever tell me what I could or couldn't achieve. No, I would do it even better. I remember the day when I came home, and my father took me aside and told me, "I'm proud of you. You're not a daughter. You're my son." It felt so good knowing that he no longer saw me as a woman but as an equal. That feeling vanished, though, the moment he returned to throwing insult after insult.

When I made it to the big boys' league, working at one of the most "competitive" jobs in one of the most "competitive" cities in the world, I was still reminded of my place and how it sucks to have XX chromosomes. You get mistaken as the assistant, or you're in the room just to take notes. You get paid less, even if you may be more qualified, so if you do want to succeed, you have to stop whining like a girl and do what the big boys do...

HUSTLE.

Shut up.

Don't complain.

Turn a deaf ear to the remarks that you're just a quota to fill.

Brag about how little sleep you got, or how much you drank,

Pretend like everything is okay even when you're bleeding.

Don't stop.

Work harder.

Work longer.

HUSTLE until everyone knows

Who has the stamina to hold out,

Who can go harder and longer than anyone else?

BIG DICK, let me hear you roar.

I didn't know what made me a woman, other than the fact that I knew I was not the only one who looked over her shoulder when walking home at night; who wondered why her body was under government purview when no man's were; or who questioned whether she was not worth an extra $0.20 like the boys.

But—at some point, I just got sick and tired of being a man.

#youtoo?

[49]

Self-Portrait, Oaxaca, Mexico, 2018

7

EYE SEE YOU

"Apartheid is a thing of the past. South Africa has evolved," a white, septuagenarian tour guide voiced over the speakers on our bus tour through Johannesburg. Days later, a visit to the township of Soweto confirmed my suspicions of how prevalent apartheid remained.

As we approached the township, the putrid smell of animal blood, waste, and smoke grew more intense. We crossed through rows of livestock carcasses that had been recently slaughtered and brought to what looked like a makeshift market. Next to the butchers, women with babies on their backs sold corn and other small vegetables. Children, barefoot and diaperless, walked across the red-stained soil in search of nothing.

Soweto had been established as a township by the South African government in the 1930s to separate Blacks and Whites. Our guide, who had grown up within the township, thanked us for visiting and told us, "Even our local police and government don't visit us here." Children surrounded me, mesmerized by my camera. When I first showed them what they looked like, they were quiet, but their shyness turned into giggles.

When I came home to review all the photos from that day's visit, I felt a tinge of shame. Had these residents wanted their photographs taken? Had I treated them just as other colonizers had and usurped their agency to be seen or unseen? Here I was, a Westerner who had come in with her new camera, shooting whatever I wanted to take. I stared at the photos I had taken of a multi-generational family sitting outside their home. The grandmother was not looking at the camera in any of the images. The grandchildren were staring at the ground, clearly uncomfortable with my presence. Who was I to take pictures of others' lives and store them in my catalog of memories as part of my "Trip to South Africa"? These were people's lives I was peering into and judging with my lens. Their stories were not mine to tell. This trip would be my introduction to the complicated narrative of photography as a medium at large.

***

Three years later, I arrived in Lebanon in the summer of 2016 amid the Syrian conflict. Even though Lebanon is barely recovering from a seventeen-year civil war and is on high alert with Israel and Hezbollah, she has kept her borders open. Of the five million in Lebanon, one million are Syrian refugees. While the abundantly resourced countries in the E.U. and the U.S. receive international aid to support the few thousand Syrian refugees at their borders, Lebanon has received no aid. The media has covered the refugee crisis at Greece and Germany's doors, but barely a word about Lebanon. Instead, the international community has left Lebanon to deal with another crisis on its own.

Many in Lebanon leave the country to seek better opportunities, but the Lebanese passport is considered the 12th worst passport to carry. Arbitrary borders that didn't exist a few decades prior now determined what you could and couldn't do.

My third trip to Lebanon proved to be the most difficult of the four visits I made. On this trip, I visited six of the most vulnerable neighborhoods in the country, the first and last of which were Palestinian settlements. As I went from neighborhood to neighborhood, my heart grew heavy. Generations of displacement kept families in holding patterns of exile. My role was to document the development of these neighborhoods as part of an ongoing U.N. Habitats survey. Entry into each of these neighborhoods required permission from the local government, and showing up in a bulletproof U.N. vehicle did not guarantee us passage.

The final neighborhood we visited was a Palestinian refugee camp in the southern region of Lebanon. This was the most arduous visit. Though we had prepared the proper paperwork to enter, the Lebanese guards were unsatisfied. After being given the runaround, we were told to go to the municipal office, where we had to get the commanding officer's permission. The administrator sat us in his office and told us to wait. He must not have gone that far because the TV in his office was still on—tuned to a Lebanese soap opera.

Half an hour later, an officer entered and sat down. He first lit a cigarette before asking me, "Why did you come to Lebanon?"

I told him the truth. "Because this country is beautiful. I love the land and people here."

"You have a Lebanese boyfriend."

I smiled.

He scribbled something on a paper napkin and handed it to me. "Here. Take this. You have my permission to go into the camp."

When we finally got past the gates, I was told to take pictures from the perimeter of the camp and that we would not be going inside the camp. *You've gotta be kidding me. We came all this way to do a survey, and we're not even going inside?* The memory of Soweto flashed before me. We can't just keep pushing populations to the edges and keep them hidden. They deserve to be seen.

"I'm going in. I'll be back in a little bit."

"If you go, you will have to assume full liability. We can't go in with you."

"Fine. I'll go in alone at my own risk. I assume full liability."

Not knowing what lay beyond the fence, I entered the camp alone. It was eerily quiet with no one around, yet I could feel eyes looking at me.

Palestinian Refugee Camp, Ain al-Hilweh, Lebanon, 2017

Moments later, I saw a woman wave to me. She seemed friendly enough. I walked towards her, trusting my gut that I'd be safe. She welcomed me and showed me around the camp with introductions to the rest of the community. She probably assumed I was either a photojournalist or an aid worker given the camera hanging around my neck.

[55]

We stopped in front of the doorway to her house, and she motioned for me to come inside. I followed her in, where I found blankets on the dirt floor, empty jugs of water, and her children playing. She opened a door—it was the bathroom. *Ma fi maai.* She pointed. "No water." Then she took me outside and pointed to the water tank. Junk, not water, was in the tank. *Ma fi maai.*

"Please take my number. Tell them we need help," she urged me. As I stood helpless, her daughter tugged on my camera and asked, *Kedili soura?*—she wanted me to take her picture. As I pulled out my camera, she ran back into the house. I thought I had scared her off, but just as fast as she had left, she returned, this time with her hijab. Once it was perfectly in place, she smiled, ready and proud for the photo. I looked back at her mother. Our eyes met. *Do you not see me*—her eyes pleaded—a mother struggling to survive, one of the thousands who had been abandoned in the middle of a political chess game. In mine, she saw her reflection—that she existed and that she deserved the same dignity as any other—to be seen.

***

I left Lebanon not long after that and arrived back in the United States quite exhausted. I had just said goodbye to the man who had been my best friend and companion for over a year, had toured the difficulties of the country, and had been torn by how easy it would be to forget all that I had seen.

A few months after adjusting to the culture shock of being back

in New York, I was invited to a fundraising event. An artist, Moral Turgeman, was doing her blind portrait project. She would look at
her subjects without looking down at her paper and draw their portrait. She was doing 10,000 of these portraits by hand as she traveled
the world. When I sat in front of her, I felt awkward and uncomfortable while she looked at me, wondering what she saw. But when she
finished my portrait, I looked down and recognized myself in it—a
confused, misplaced, tired being. Just by sitting with me in silence and
looking directly into my eyes, she had seen me.

I had been reading Susan Sontag's *On Photography,* which raised
questions about the ethics and power dynamics of photography. Colo-
nialists used their cameras to shoot the colonized and bring back tro-
phy images that fanned the fears of white viewers back home. What
role did photography have other than propaganda if the oppressed remained subjects of the oppressors' lens? Did Sharbat Gula want to be
Steve McCurry's "Afghan girl"? How could we move away from sen-
sationalism and run towards connection?

I drew inspiration from Maral's portrait project and Sontag's essays
and started the Eye See You Project. I removed any predatory photo-
graphic language, taking out words such as "shoot," "subject" and "cap-
ture" and explained to participants that we would be co-creating our
photo session together. Before I would pick up my camera, I would
share the inspiration for the project and my experiences in South Africa and Lebanon. Almost everyone shared a story from their own
heart, and that's how each session would begin.

I had no end goal for this project, other than to photograph 1,000 strangers. I figured I could fund and complete this project by myself, but it took on a life of its own. The first activation of Eye See You occurred spontaneously at my friends' holiday pop-up market. Kytzia and Yoyo encouraged me to share my project there. One of the women I photographed that evening, Juanita, became one of my biggest advocates and collaborators. That encounter changed the course of the project altogether.

She shared that she was planning a dinner experience called I See You. The idea had been inspired by her time volunteering in Greece at a refugee camp. I shared the background of the Eye See You Project I was doing, and right then and there we decided to incorporate the portraits as part of the I See You dinner.

The first I See You dinner was attended by Rodrigo, the founder of The Assemblage, New York's newest coworking / co-living community. I overheard Juanita encouraging Rodrigo to sit with me for a portrait. "I think you'll enjoy the experience."

As Rodrigo sat reluctantly in front of my camera, I could feel nerves flooding my body. But when I picked up the camera and began looking into his eyes, the tension inside of me softened. He was so moved by the experience that he said, "This is exactly what we need to have at The Assemblage."

Less than a week later, I got a message from the VP of Marketing at The Assemblage asking to speak to me about the Eye See You Project. They wanted to commission me to do 250 member portraits. I couldn't believe what I was hearing. 250 portraits? Not only that, but they were going to promote the project to their community and give

me the space to do the portraits. This would be the first of many spon-
sorships for the Eye See You Project.

A few weeks later, I hosted a Korean New Year dinner at my apartment. Over dinner, all the guests expressed what they were grateful
for and what their intentions were for the upcoming year. When my
turn arrived, I shared how trying the last three years had been for me.
I had not yet found my confidence in photography and had been sec-
ond-guessing my decision to quit my job. But with the Eye See You
Project, I knew I hadn't been wandering aimlessly. Amongst the guests
was the founder of a tech company. After hearing my story and the
photos on my wall, Francis said, "Let's set up a call and connect next
week. I have a project for you." Five minutes into our meeting, he
said, "Will you do 100 portraits and bios for us the Eye See You way?"
I blinked, shocked by what I was hearing. I hadn't even pitched to anyone, and now two major sponsors had fallen into my lap.

Not long after, a Brazilian footwear brand invited me to do an Eye
See You pop-up experience in their downtown SoHo shop and display the portraits on their huge LCD screen on Broadway so passersby
could see. What was happening? I was in complete shock. I still didn't
believe that I was a photographer, despite getting these huge endorse-
ments.

Other photographers collaborated with me to help complete the
project. One of them included the former editor of *National Geograph-
ic Brazil*. When she sent me a message asking to speak with me, I was
so afraid something had gone wrong. Instead, she shared how powerful the portrait experience had been for her and that she wanted to

[59]

share what she experienced. An editor of Nat Geo was telling me this was the first time in 20 years that she had experienced photographing like this. Come again? "It was so different to be photographing in this way. After eyegazing for five minutes, the whole dynamics between us changed. He helped me set up the lights, and we made the scene for the portrait *together*."

The meeting with the woman and her family in the Palestinian refugee camp had woken something in me. That single encounter became the catalyst for the Eye See You Project. In the span of a few months, I had gone to the Philippines, Brazil, Kenya, Mexico, Lebanon, and Black Rock City with that project. The project was unfolding on its own. I used to think that I had to hustle as hard as I could to get a project off the ground, but with the Eye See You Project, I discovered that I didn't have to do what the big boys do. All I had to do was show up and trust the creative process.

After I had started the Eye See You Project, I discovered that the tribes of northern Natal in South Africa greet one another with *sawabona*. The transliteration is "I see you," as in, "I respect and acknowledge you for who you are." The response to this is *sikbona*, which translates to, "I am here," or in other words, "When you see me you bring me into existence."

This project taught me that everyone has a story and that in taking a few moments to hear someone else's, I could remember who I was.
***

In 2018, Rodrigo organized a weekend retreat for friends in upstate

New York. Other than our interaction with the Eye See You Project, we hadn't spoken much. When we sat next to each other around the bonfire, he turned to me and said, "I see you." Looking more intently at me, he repeated the words, "I see you." I got chills. Had he been able to see through my relapse with my meds or was he acknowledging the work I was doing? I didn't know how to react to his comment. All I knew was that I was not alone in his gaze.

A few years later, Rodrigo transitioned from this world, and the news of his passing shook me. Cancer had returned, and I had not told him what he meant to me. *Rodrigo~ sikbona.*

Eye See You Portrait of Rodrigo, New York, 2018

8

GANESHA

I'm back at my parents' home for the holidays when my mother comes into my room with a look of deep concern. She wants to talk.

"I am so disappointed," she says.

"What happened?"

"You are praying to another god."

"Another god? What god?" I ask, clueless.

Then I remembered I had forgotten to put my altar. Alongside my crystals, prayer beads, a St. Christopher pendant, evil eye, medicine pouch, and sage, I have a card with a picture of Ganesha and a verse from the Bhagavad Gita. I had broken commandment numero dos: Thou shalt not have any other gods before me. I had forgotten to put my altar away to avoid this exact conversation, but it was too late.

"It's just a picture, Mom. I'm not actually praying to it."

"If you're not praying to that card, then who are you praying to?"

"God," I reply.

"Who is your god?"

I remained silent, knowing there was only one possible way this conversation would end, but she kept poking me. "You don't even go to church. How can you say you believe in God?"

"Mom, I pray to the same God as you. How I pray just looks different," I snap.

"You're just like your sister. What a disappointment."

Her judgment triggers a deep wound in me. Religious differences split my family apart. I still remember the night my sister and her then-boyfriend met with my parents. In this Korean household, boyfriends don't come around unless it's serious. It's "disrespectful" to introduce your parents to someone less than proposal material. The other rule in our household is that you had to get married in the Catholic church. This rule would be problematic for my sister, seeing that her boyfriend was Seventh Day Adventist and that my sister refused to have her future husband convert to Catholicism. In fact, she had begun attending service at his church, which drove my mother mad.

The following morning, I woke up with a sick feeling in my stomach. Something was off. My sister was not at home, and when I asked my mother what was wrong, she kept silent. Born 13 years after my brother, I was the baby in the family, often kept in the dark about "adult" things." But I could sense that something serious had happened. Later, my brother explained that my father had disowned my sister.

"What does that mean?" I asked.

"She's not allowed to come home," my brother said.

"But why? Did she do something wrong?"

"She's getting married without Dad's permission."

My eight-year-old brain could not understand. A year earlier, my eldest sister had gotten married, and her getting married was one of the happiest memories I had as a kid. I rarely got to spend time with my big sisters because they were already in university by the time I could speak. But with all the wedding preparations, I got to spend time with the both of them doing "adult" things, tagging along wherever they went. I had my two sisters all to myself. In the backseat, I drew wedding dresses and showed my sisters what I had drawn. "Wow, you're so creative," they responded. Whenever I showed my mother any of my drawings, she'd tell me, "I'm busy," and shoo me away. I treasured every moment I had with my sisters.

But now, I couldn't even mention my sister's name. Our home had become a house of eggshells. My father forbade my mother from going to the wedding. If she did not obey, he would divorce her. I got the message: if you choose your sister, you won't be loved.

My mother wasn't the only one who had to choose sides. When my sister asked me to be the flower girl for her wedding, my stomach churned. I feared what my father might say or how we would punish me, but I was only eight years old and wanted to be there for my sister.

After I came home from the rehearsal dinner, the night before my sister's big day, my father announced that I could not go to the wedding. As the flower girl, I thought my presence make my sister feel less sad about my parents' absence. But now, I wouldn't be there. Who would walk with her down the aisle? It was less than 12 hours before the wedding, and I knew the news that I couldn't come would be another blow for my sister.

That night, I cried harder than I ever had. No one in my family cried, at least not that I had seen. Not because they didn't feel anything but because any sign of weakness left them vulnerable. And in this family, you had to keep your guard up, always at the ready for an attack. At one point, my sobs were so loud that my oldest sister told me to lower my voice, or else my father... All she had to do was mention my father, and I knew what she meant. The silent tears that soaked my pillow that night were for all of us.

When I woke, the house was silent. My mother had gone to work, and my father had gone golfing like any other day. My other sister and brother had already left for the wedding. Why they had been allowed to go to the wedding didn't make much sense to me, but I came up with my own theories. My father couldn't tell my oldest sister what to do anymore because she was married and no longer living under my father's rules. By the time I was eight, I had concluded that marriage may have been a prison, but it could also be an escape route from my father. As for my brother, I figured he got to attend because he's a boy— those double standards again.

My middle sister and her husband moved to San Diego a few months after getting married, yet I hardly saw her. On occasion, my other siblings would sneak me away to see her while my father was away. Visits with my sister usually accompanied terrible stomach aches. My anxiety was high. I was only nine years old, having to choose between two people I loved— my father and my sister. In some ways, I can relate to children of divorce.

Two years went by before my father and sister spoke to each other. I remember that day as if it were yesterday. My sister and brother-in-law took me out on a mini fishing excursion. When we decided to head back to the docks, the boat's motor blew out. We were stuck in the middle of the lake. I tried to remain calm, but all I could think of was how much trouble I'd get in if I wasn't home before my dad arrived. My mother and sister had arranged things to make sure I was back before my father came home. As luck would have it, my brother-in-law had to row us all the way back to shore. I was definitely going to be home late.

My sister and brother-in-law dropped me off and watched me from the car as I rang the doorbell. When my mother opened the door, I was relieved, but before I could head to my room, I saw my father sitting at the dinner table in clear sight. I had been caught. As I prepared myself for a chew-out, my father said, "Tell them to come inside and have dinner."

Frozen in surprise, I looked to my mother to make sure I had heard him correctly, but she had already begun walking to their car, and by the time I understood what was happening, my sister and brother-in-law were taking off their shoes to come inside. My sister had gotten into a car accident a few months prior, and my father had not even called to check in on her, nor had my mother been able to see her daughter in the hospital. After two years of completely denying her existence, my father was offering my sister dinner.

He did not say a single word about the wedding. He carried on a conversation as though nothing had ever happened. It would take nearly 18 years for my father to acknowledge the pain he had caused. Some would say better late than never, but the damage had already been done: I no longer trusted my father, and I learned from an early age that love was conditional.

That's how our family dealt with religious differences.

***

When my mother demanded to know which god I prayed to, I wish I could have expressed what the prayer card she feared so much meant to me.

I received the card from Liza, my yoga teacher. She gave it to me right before I went on my year of travels after quitting my job. Daily Ashtanga practice at her Garage Yoga Shala helped me gain the strength and grounding I needed during this rocky transition.

The Ashtanga Mysore practice is a devotional one practiced six days a week, except on new and full moon days or during menstruation. Students are to come to the mat no matter what. Even when injured, we still came and modified our practice as needed. Some days I flew through the poses, and on some, I spontaneously broke into tears. As Bessel van der Kolk would say, "The body keeps the score."

Liza, Garage Yoga Shala, San Diego, California, 2016

On the back of the card is a verse from the Bhagavad Gita, Chapter 2, Verse 69, which reads:

"What all beings consider as day is the night of ignorance for the wise, and what all creatures see as night is the day for the introspective sage."

There are different transliterations of this Sanskrit verse, but I've come to understand this passage as a call to embrace the unknown, the darkness. It reminds me that equanimity and mystery go hand-in-hand.

Ganesha is traditionally depicted with sweets in one hand (which

[69]

looks more like a bowl of rice to me), a rosary in another, with a rat sitting in front of the deity. In many ways, I saw a likeness between Ganesha and my mother. My mother's love language is food. She did not hug or encourage us, but she loved us with her hands. She cooked every day for the family and made sure everyone else was fed before she would sit down to eat. But there are a few distinct memories I have of her eating for herself.

One summer, my mother and I took a trip to visit our family in South Korea. We went down by the piers, and as we walked by the vendors selling fish, she stopped at one of the stands and ordered food. She asked for sea urchin and abalone. The vendor grabbed several urchins from the water and began preparing them, and then moved on to the abalone. Korean mothers are notorious for piling food on your plate without even asking. You think you're finished, but then comes another piece of fish or another heap of rice. I thought she would nag me for not eating, but my mother didn't say a word. Bite after bite, she dipped the abalone in red chili paste and ate uninterrupted. I had never seen her so relaxed and carefree. "You know, your grandfather, my father, used to love abalone. Growing up, we'd...," she began telling me. She rarely spoke about her past, but as she ate, I learned so much about my mother. She wasn't just my *umma* ("mom" in Korean), she was a little girl who had stories of her own.

The other memory I have was when she came to visit me in Washington D.C. to help me with my wedding preparations. I decided to take her out for brunch at José Andrés's Café Atlantico, the fine dining restaurant where I had been working part-time. It was here I was introduced to the world of molecular gastronomy. It was a gamble taking my mother there, not knowing if she would enjoy the foams and gels—plus it was a 20-course brunch. Mealtimes were stressful for her. She cooked every day and nearly every meal, and it was about a 50% hit rate whether my father would complain. Fights usually started around the dinner table. Depending on how hangry or stressed my father was that day, he'd either love the food or hate it. If the latter, duck, because plates may come flying across the room.

At Café Atlantico, the chef, my manager, and the rest of the staff treated my mother as a guest of honor. She had never had such a dining experience. On course number 10, with 10 more to go, I nervously asked my mother if she liked the food. As she took the shell off the prawn she said, "I've never been able to experience food like this. You know how your father is. I can't go anywhere with him." Then she put the prawn in her mouth and chewed with the same content as she had with the sea urchin and abalone.

Even though none of my family members see eye to eye on religion, in some twisted way, it's what ties us together. Everyone in my family prays, even my somewhat agnostic brother. We grew up watching my mother pray the rosary daily. After waking up in the morning, she'd take me to school, work a ten-hour day, come home to cook dinner for the family, work on whatever else she needed to do for her church obligations, and then like clockwork, she'd find the time at the end of the night to sit in prayer with her rosary beads—the same that Ganesha held in the image.

Below Ganesha sits a rat. The presence of this tiny creature is a reminder of Ganesha's mighty abilities to remove and overcome all obstacles. Like Ganesha, my mother removed obstacles, including my father, who was born in the year of the rat. When my father said no to voice lessons, my mother gave me money anyways and told me to go sing. Or if I wanted to go on a trip with friends, my mom would talk to my father for me. When my sister was excommunicated, it was my mother who snuck me out to see her.

I'd like a do-over of the conversation I had with her that day. I would start by telling her that I had no idea what unacknowledged sacrifices she had to make to keep our family together, nor was it my place to judge her or resent her for why she did. Whether my life would have been better or worse had she left my father did not matter. I could either stay focused on the rat or take responsibility for my life and overcome as the image of Ganesha reminded me.

Instead of getting frustrated, I would tell her that I pray because of her; she taught me how to have faith and persevere even when nothing made sense. I'd tell her that this card has traveled with me across the U.S., back and forth from New York to California. It's also been with me to Lebanon, Turkey, Kenya, and the Philippines. It's traveled south to Mexico and Brazil, and all the way back north to Texas. It's been with me on all my travels, reminding me that as I move through the unknown, there is nothing prayer cannot answer.

Coming back to her question, "Who is your god?" I'd tell her it's the presence I feel when I'm photographing or the spaces between breaths when I'm on my yoga mat, or the source that pulses through the rivers and winds. Photography is my prayer. Everything I sense in the scene before me all comes into focus. Yoga is my prayer. All the beads of sweat from asana practice would make hundreds of rosaries. My daily morning dance is my twirling devotion. When I write, I know that Spirit is with me to the *t*. And the list goes on, for life is my prayer.

One of my many prayer altars, Lisbon, Portugal, 2022

[73]

9

SADDLE UP

Val and I met in yoga teacher training and became fast friends. She is an outdoor-loving med school student who has a greater appetite for adventure and a more curious mind than anyone I've ever met. We spent time together at the rock climbing gym, going to yoga classes, or running (when I wasn't feeling embarrassed about how slow I ran compared to Val, the athlete of the century). It took less than five minutes to bike to one another's homes in Windansea, La Jolla. Together we threw dinner parties, one of which we spent a whole two days preparing for, making kombu for our very own ramen. We may have nailed the broth, but I'm afraid the noodles were questionable. Nevertheless, it was a triumph in experimentation.

One night after working up a good sweat salsa dancing, Val and I got on our bikes, heels still on, and rode up Mount Soledad, where you can see all of San Diego. That late-night ride inspired us to plan one final epic hurrah together—a ride down the Pacific Coast from Portland to San Diego. In a few months, both of us would be leaving the West Coast for our respective grad school programs on the East Coast. The difference was that Val knew where she was going, while I still had a decision to make. Two MBA programs had accepted me. One was a full-ride scholarship to my backup school, and the other was my dream school, with no financial support.

Rather than feeling proud that I had been accepted to two programs, I grew anxious over the thought of having to choose a program. The last major life decision I made ended in divorce. Could I trust myself to choose wisely? Decision-making crippled me. A whole drama would play before me in the frozen section at the grocery store over which Ben & Jerry's flavor to get. Cherry Garcia or Chunky Monkey? *If you don't pick the right one, you could have another divorce on your hands. Don't mess this up, or else...*

***

Through sun and rain, Val and I worked our way down the coast of Oregon. Many coastal roads had only one lane with no shoulder, so we had to share the road with 24-foot trucks that would nearly scrape us off the road. In the first two days of our ride, we had covered 140 miles. Everything in my body was sore from the first two days of riding, especially my legs and glutes. The padding in my riding shorts proved insufficient for my bony Asian ass, so I rolled up my towel and stuffed them into my shorts. What a relief. I can do this ride, I thought, but on the third day of our journey, we would climb one of the steepest hills of our adventure. No amount of padding in my seat would get me through the next hour of ascent. My legs were too tired to stand up and pedal, so I pedaled with butt in saddle, crawling slower than a snail. I pedaled the bare minimum so I wouldn't tip over in my clip-ins, but the black asphalt hardly changed shape.

Sure, I could carry the weight of my body and two paneers, but a load of anxiety over which graduate program to choose was weighing me down. With every yellow line on the road, my decision would change. Do I take the full-ride scholarship or pay full tuition for my dream school? (First-world problems, I know, but the familial pressure was real.) I looked ahead and couldn't see Val. By now, she was probably zipping through the next town. *G, right now, you need to focus on getting up this hill. The sun is not going to wait for you all day. Drop it.* With that, I began breathing, *Left, Right, Left, Right.*

I don't know how much time passed before the trees canopying above slowly started to thin. I lifted my head. *What the...?* I had made it to the top of the hill. Outstretched before me, I could see a flock of birds gliding above the Pacific Ocean. It was all downhill from here. I kept the momentum, *Left, Right, Left, Right.*

Out from the shade of the trees, now under direct sunlight, I flew down the Pacific. Clocking in at 40+ mph, I stopped cycling and let the tailwind send me flying downhill. At this speed, a small pebble or pothole could have been the end of my ride, but I kept my eyes on the birds cresting the waves. I wanted to ride along with them. *Yee-haw, I* let out.

When I got to the bottom of the hill, all the anxiety about grad school vanished. Val and I pulled over to the side of the road and stared at the ocean. "Damn, we did it."

What I learned on that ride was no matter the road I took, I would get up and fly. All I had to do was stay in the saddle and put one foot in front of the other.

Left, Right, Left, Right.

Pacific Coast Highway, Oregon, 2012

10

LOST IN THE DESERT

I had been driving nearly all day through the mountains, mesmerized by the vastness of the land. Stretches of land extended farther than the eye could see. I hadn't done much planning for this trip except allowing my curiosity to guide me. I had four general destinations in mind—ride through the dunes of Oman, discover the shores of the Arabian Gulf, wade in the wadis, and get lost in the mountains.

It was starting to get late, and I was behind on my driving schedule. How could there be such land that lifted pink dust from the ground to cover the ivory rocks so softly? The light was unlike any other light I had seen. Every dozen or so kilometers, another terrain or contour would emerge, and I'd pull over to photograph—a perfect distraction from the tears I had cried the prior evening.

Jebel Shams, Oman, 2017

But with the sun starting to set, I knew that this was not the time to dilly dally. It was now about 15:00, and I still had at least another three or four hours to drive before my next destination—a camp in the middle of the desert. I said my goodbyes to the mountains and set my camera down to focus on the long drive through the endless pristine roads of Oman.

The sun had long said goodbye, and I was now left with the light of my GPS guiding me to the camp. According to the map, I was only a few kilometers away. All I had to do was pass through this small town, and I would be there, soon enough—so I thought.

Once I got to the town, I planned to ask a local to point me in the direction of the camp. Surely, someone would know where it hid. The shadows rolled back into the artificial blue streetlights, and I found myself in a pueblo of sorts. Outside, men were gathered around wooden tables, drinking tea on overturned buckets acting as makeshift seats. I looked from left to right and realized that getting out of the car to ask for directions would not be smart. My tendency to overlook sketchy situations like riding the F train in the wee hours in New York slowly began to wane. Sure, I could handle a few wild characters on the F train, but I didn't want to risk drawing attention as the lone woman in a town full of men. There were no women out that night. In fact, throughout much of my journey in Oman, I had seen very few women.

Not wanting to offend the customs of the land, I passed through the town without asking for directions. I would have to figure out another way to camp. I pulled over in an alley and looked around to see if perhaps I could find another path on the map. I turned on my cellphone service and made an international roaming call to contact my host. Fuck it if it cost $3 per minute. I was starving, tired, and desperate to get to camp.

The phone rang.

No response.

I tried again.

Still no response.

Just wait. There's no point in panicking. Just wait.

That's when I heard the voice of the sun. *I warned you earlier to put your camera down and drive, yet you decided that you would stay with me until the end. Now I cannot be here with you, as I must go to the other side of the world. Now you must wait here in the darkness.*

Twenty minutes later, my phone rang. "Genevieve?"

"Yes, that's me."

"Hi. I'm your host. Where are you now?"

"I'm not sure, but the GPS says I'm close. Can you help me?"

"Yes, I will send someone to meet you. You must go to the gas station down the road."

As I mentally retraced the blank road I had been traveling, I recalled seeing a gas station kilometers back. Could that possibly be the one? In poor Arabic, I asked, "El Maha gas station?"

"Yes, go there. We will send someone to meet you."

It was 20:45, and I could barely think straight. I hadn't eaten all day, and I had to go to the bathroom. Worst case scenario, I could go to the gas station and relieve myself. The highway leading to the gas station was silent. It was as though I was the only person awake. Where was everyone? Was there some holiday or curfew I did not know about?

About 15 kilometers later, I saw a gas station in the distance. That must be it. I pulled up to the gas station and found myself in an even more precarious situation. This was the only business open and the only light I could see for miles. In front of me was a sea of blackness and behind me was nothing but faint silhouettes of a road leading nowhere. The town full of men I had passed through seemed less daunting than this lone-lit gas station.

What had I gotten myself into? Was this reckless traveling on my part? Or was it the medicine I needed for my ailing heart? While sitting in the parking lot of the gas station, I saw headlights in the distance and heard the faint sound of music. The brighter the headlights became, the louder the music and revelry grew. A Toyota pickup truck pulled up with a truck bed filled with men. This was not my host. It was now 21:30, and time was ticking.

Just re-park the car in the dark. No one will be able to see you. As I began to move the car to hide from the men, another car pulled up. What was this gas station? Had my host asked to meet me here to corner me? My nerves were raw from all the crying I had done earlier in the day. No matter how much I wanted it to work between the two of us, my heart knew it was time for us to go our separate ways. When I would get back from Oman, we'd have to have the painful conversation we were avoiding. This is not the time to start crying. Focus on finding shelter.

When the second car pulled up next to me, a man rolled down his window and asked, "Genevieve?"

"Yes?"

"I am here to take you to the camp." The sigh of relief that came over me was short-lived with his next statement.

"Have you ever driven through dunes before?"

"No."

"Okay. First, we need to take out the air from your tires."

I recalled reading on one of the travel forums that lowering the tire pressure would allow for more control while riding through the dunes. It made sense, but this would leave me with a vehicle incapable of escape.

In asking me to release air from my tires, he was also asking me to release the last bit of control I had. *Let out the air from my tires so that I can let you take me through some dunes in the middle of nowhere to a camp I've never seen before?* But, the kindness in the man's eyes encouraged me to surrender.

"Okay, follow me. I drive slow."

We rolled out of the gas station, and less than a kilometer later, we pulled off the highway and headed onto a dirt road. There was no way I could have navigated my way to camp on my own. This off-road pull-off appeared out of nowhere.

The first few kilometers were paved with enough gravel for me to feel confident. *This isn't so difficult. I can handle this.* But as we traveled, farther along, the distance between my guide's car and mine grew further, and the dusty road cut my visibility to only a few meters ahead. The dance of terrain and tire began. As we curved and turned, I could feel the ground below me turn to mush and slip underneath me. My guide was far ahead of me, and I could barely see his taillights.

As I looked to my right, I tall silhouettes. After allowing my eyes to adjust, I realized I was driving past a wall of rolling dunes. When I looked ahead, my host was nowhere to be seen. *Just keep driving.* Even though I should have been focused on the road ahead, I couldn't help but look to my right, hypnotized by the contours of the dunes. The waves of sand in Death Valley felt petite in comparison to the fortress of dunes out here.

My concentration broke when I saw two red lights. My host's car had stopped. He got out of the car and motioned me to slow down. "We have to let out more pressure from your tires."

Before I could ask him any questions, I heard hissing noises. He had released more air from my tires.

"Drive straight. We go down. Then press gas hard, okay?"

"Can you say that again?"

"Drive fast. Don't slow down."

Don't slow down? I didn't have much time to process this because he was already back in his car and driving fast ahead. I pressed on the gas and did my best to follow right behind him, but no sooner did I see him ascend and then disappear. There I was, alone in the darkness, hydroplaning to who knows where. As I went down the dip, I instinctually pressed on the gas, feeling the car slip under me. And as I pressed ahead, I spiraled out of control only to press on the brakes in time, right next to my guide's car. He pointed ahead to a campfire with tents circled. We arrived. I stepped out of the car and looked up at the sky. I couldn't believe how many stars I saw. No light pollution. *I've arrived.* My host already had my bag and began walking toward the camp.

"Am I the only one here?"

"No, but you are the last to arrive this evening. We have prepared dinner for you. I will put your bags in your tent for you. Please sit and eat."

I sat in silence under the tent with a view of the dunes and the speckled night sky.

As I sat to eat this solitary meal, it became apparent how lonely I had been while traveling, and how much I no longer wanted to do it alone. But who would I be able to travel with? That was still unknown.

"Tomorrow, at 4 a.m., meet at the back of your tent. Your guide will be there then."

The silence of the desert night drove me mad. My worries about the inevitable grew louder. When I got into my tent, I immediately called Desiree. "Des, I think this is the end for us. We love each other, but it's time for us to go our separate ways."

"Yes, your next conversation with him will be a turning point."

For nearly a year, the two of us had not discussed the future, and with one of us based in New York and the other based in Beirut, we danced around the subject. When we were together, though, we took turns cooking, danced late into the evening, watched the stars, rolled Js, joked about nothing, left each other voice note after voice note, and loved each other. He, my daily dose of sunshine, and I, his supernova.

As soon as the tears on my face had time to dry, it was time to get up for the next leg of the journey.

"Miss, it's time to go."

It was barely 4 a.m., and the sun had not risen. No one would be able to see my tear-swollen eyes.

In the dark, I followed the voice of my guide. With a flashlight, I saw two camels. Up I went on the back of one. We rode until the night turned purple, at which point we stopped and got off our camels. We sat as purple turned pink. The blushing sky yawned with oranges and yellows as the sun rose.

Though everything in me wished for a fast-forward button, I knew I had to write this chapter to its end.

Back up on the camel, we rode into the sun. In the distance, I saw the silhouette of a lone camel. I wasn't sure where it was going, but I knew it was exactly where it was meant to be.

***

On my last night in Oman, I found an artisanal shop filled with beautiful ceramics. Amongst them were handcrafted camels that reminded me of the one I had seen in the distance. I asked the store clerk to wrap it carefully to ensure that it would make the turbulent trip back. It was the one thing I had to hold on to before I let go.

The camel is a beautiful spirit. It is one of sojourn, endurance, and perseverance. Across deserts and in harsh conditions, this creature can withstand the elements of life, just as we had in our sojourn together. I gave the camel to him before we said goodbye. I knew he alone would take good care of the camel.

***

Three years later, in 2020, an explosion in Beirut devastates the entire city. When I hear the news, I immediately call him. No answer. I leave a voice note: "I just heard about the explosion. Let me know if you're okay."

A few hours later, I get a message from him. "I'm okay. We're actually in Dubai. I'll call you when I get back." He sends me photos that his neighbor had taken of his apartment. Destroyed. He had just bought this apartment not long ago.

A few days later, he called me from his family's home. A few workers had gone to his apartment in Beirut to pick up some of his things. "You have no idea how happy it made me see the camel had survived the blast. Quack Quack made it too, but I expected her to survive a blast. A ceramic camel, though?" We laughed. Quack Quack was a rubber duck I had given him as an inside joke, memories of a summer spent floating together.

Months later, we're on a video call, and he gives me a tour of his renovated apartment. "Do you see it?" On his living room mantel, I could see the camel was still standing.

Wahiba Sands Desert, Oman, 2017

11

GRECIA AND ME

When Eduardo asked if I wanted to sleep in the barn with the horses, I said yes before I could even blink.

That same afternoon the stablehands hung a hammock in one of the horse stalls.

"Whose stall is this?" I asked Eduardo.

"Grecia's," he said with a grin.

I couldn't remember which one was Grecia. There were so many horses on the farm.

"She's one of the horses you photographed in the chapel," he reminded me.

Three months earlier, the Instagram algorithm gods had brought Eduardo into my life. He asked to have coffee so he could share a photo project he had in mind. Before saying yes to coffee, the skeptic in me replied, "Can you tell me a little more about the project first?"

He wrote back, "I am planning to take you to Brazil to take pictures of my horses. Horses are usually pictured as objects and not souls. I want pictures that can go deep into the wild spirit of the horse and heart. I believe you can do that."

For years I had held in my heart a photo that Eve Arnold, one of the only women photographers to be a member of the prestigious Magnum photojournal collective, had made. Underneath a cloudless blue sky lay a white horse and a girl dressed in pink, set in the middle of the vast grasslands of Mongolia. Maybe this would be my opportunity.

I wasn't sure if he was serious, but I needed coffee anyway. Why not, I thought.

We met at Buvette in the West Village, and over breakfast, Eduardo shared the story of how he came to love horses. His grandfather, a larger-than-life intimidating figure, noticed Eduardo's natural talent with horses and bought him his first horse. Through horses, he saw the tender side of his grandfather, and a bond grew between them. His grandfather's love helped Eduardo grow into a champion breeder of the Mangalarga Marchador, Brazil's pride and national horse. With the recent passing of his grandfather and the many other challenges in his heart—including marriage, separation, and miscarriage—he was reevaluating what was most precious to him.

"I want to explore themes around the wildness of the heart, from the love I received from my grandfather and the beauty and power of the horses to the transgressions we choose in life. There are so many stories we can tell. One idea I have is to bring the horses into the chapel on the fazenda."

As he spoke, I could already see the story coming to life. We'd be unraveling the institutions of domestication and conditioning, and returning to a place of the wild. This project wasn't just for Eduardo; it would be for all of us to connect to our nature, untamed and free. "Amen," I said. "I'd be honored to do this project with you."

***

As the stable hands finished setting up the hammock, I said, "Of course, I remember *Grecia*." She had been one of the horses selected for the chapel scene. I hadn't spent much time with horses prior to this project, so I didn't know what to expect. Every frame I set up took quite a bit of time. We had to direct the horses in the right spot, but trying to move them in a tiny chapel is no small feat. When we did get the horses in the right position, the shot would be shit. Turns out, you can't ask a horse to model for more than 20 minutes before one of them decides to take a dump. So after clean-up, we'd have to try to reposition the horses and set the scene again.

Fazenda Pao Grande, Brazil, 2019

Later that evening, I gathered all my gear from the main house and walked to the barn in the darkness. The entire staff had already gone

[93]

home, so it was just the horses and me on the estate. When I arrived in front of Grecia's stall, it dawned on me that maybe she didn't want me in her space. I hadn't asked her if she was okay with a sleepover. But she was probably used to that from humans. We don't ask for permission. Instead, we seize and destroy until we've got no planet left.

Before entering the stall, I introduced myself to Grecia and the other horses in the barn. "Hey ladies, I hope you don't mind that I'll be staying with you tonight. Grecia, if it's alright with you, I'd like to sleep in your room tonight. It might be a little tight, but I promise to be a good guest and clean up after myself."

With that, I entered the space.

As I adjusted the blankets and organized my camera gear in the hammock, Grecia began circling me, pushing the hammock side to side.

"What are you doing here?" she motioned. As I lay down in the hammock, Grecia continued her inspection, now nipping and chewing the hammock. She had every right to frisk the intruder. Over in the next stall, I could see her friend Gaffiera peering through the opening to inspect the night visitor. She was curious about what I was doing in Grecia's stall and likely keeping watch of her friend. I resigned that I would not be sleeping much that night.

But almost immediately after I had this thought, Grecia began slowing her movements. She positioned her head over the hammock, right where my lap was, and I could smell the sweetness of her breath. Grass and field. I began petting her forehead and breathed with her.

After some time, her head began to lower, and now her chin was resting on my lap. When I removed my hand from her forehead, Grecia remained still, leaving her chin in my lap. I could feel the hammock growing taut. Grecia had fallen asleep in my lap. Silence befell the barn; at last, I closed my eyes.

The chill of the night woke me hours later. It was cold, and the blankets I had brought were not warm enough for winter nights in a barn. I looked around for Grecia, but I could not see her. Where was she? Had I left the stall gate open? I sat up to look around for her and discovered her lying on the bed of hay sound asleep.

Horses sleep on average four hours a day, and they mostly do so standing to stay alert for predators. In her stall, sleeping alongside her was one of the most destructive predators on the planet. Tears rolled down my cheeks. I whispered to Grecia, "We barely know each other, but thank you for trusting me. Thank you for your unconditional love."

I woke up again at about 5 a.m. and returned to my bed. My body could no longer handle the cold. Grecia was already up, talking to Gaffiera in the other stall. I could only imagine what they were talking about after last night.

That morning Grecia and four other horses would be traveling to make their way to Brazil's annual national horse competition in Belo Horizonte. This event was the apex of all the training the horses had prepared.

A week later, I followed suit and flew to Belo Horizonte to attend the competition. It was the biggest week for all of Brazil's Mangalarga Marchador community. I was in shock seeing how many horses and people were in attendance. What a show. It was like Burning Man for horses. Makeshift camps here and there with horses and teams from farms all over the country.

The entire Fazenda Pao Grande team was in attendance: Eduardo, the horse trainers, the veterinarian, and even Eduardo's father. It had always been Eduardo's grandfather who went to the shows, and this was the first time his father had attended. It was beautiful to witness this new chapter unfolding for Eduardo.

After lunch, I asked Eduardo if we could visit Grecia. I wondered whether she would remember me. Was I the only one who had felt the connection that night? Would she have allowed just anyone to sleep beside her? As we approached Grecia's stall, I slowed my walk to observe her from a distance. She was eating in the back corner with her rear facing me. As I got closer, she looked up from her pile of hay, stopped chewing, and turned around to face me. Then she walked towards me to the front of the stall.

"It took you long enough to get here. Geez, did you come by horse?" she asked with her nose and licks.

It was the best greeting she could have given me.

"Can I go into her stall?" I asked Mu, the horse trainer who had helped with the hammock.

"Of course!" he smiled.

I opened the gate, and Grecia immediately began smelling me and nudging me to pet her.

I hugged her with everything inside me. When I let go, she continued to nip at my arm, so I thought maybe she wanted me to leave her alone. I moved to the other side of the stall, but she followed me. I wasn't sure if she was trying to push me out, so I moved to the other corner. Wherever I moved, she followed. Maybe she wasn't trying to corner me. I asked a horse trainer later what her movements may have meant, and she explained, "Horses are herd animals. They move together. She was following you because she considers you as part of her herd."

The horse totem represents power, freedom, and heart. Horse spirit calls us to embrace endurance, journey, and intuition. Grecia was here to remind me that the way forward was through unconditional love—to accept both the prey and predator aspects of myself. She showed me that through vulnerability, we can meet our shadows and still fall in love.

Fazenda Pao Grande, Rio de Janeiro, Brazil, 2019

12

MEDS

"If you are experiencing difficulty or think you might have depression, do not be embarrassed. There are campus psychologists who can help you," my biology professor stated. He was a renowned researcher for the National Institute of Health who had been silently struggling for years with depression. After years of research, he concluded that neurochemical imbalances were nothing to be ashamed of, and he began devoting his life to researching and destigmatizing depression and other mental illnesses. Hence that day's dedicated lecture on depression. Projected on the screen:

Anger.

Lack of focus.

Brain fog.

Apathy.

Low to no sex drive.

Social withdrawal.

As I continued reading the list of symptoms, I wasn't sure what to feel—relief or shame. In *Atlas of the Heart,* Brene Brown discusses how important language is in understanding and changing our world. Before reading the symptoms, I thought depression meant non-stop crying, which did not include me. I had every other symptom, though. On the one hand, giving language to my experiences offered a dose of comfort and confirmation that I wasn't the only one dealing with these issues; on the other hand, I felt ashamed of all my defects.

"If you need help, there are campus psychologists who can help," my professor repeated. I had told my then-husband that I wanted to get some help, but he told me that if others found out just how crazy I was, I'd get locked up in a loony bin. For my sake, it would be best for me not to see a therapist. My professor's voice drowned out my ex's, and after that lecture, I scheduled an appointment to see one of the school psychologists.

After that visit, I had a good long look at myself in the mirror and began my journey to recovery.

***

Cabrillo Bridge, San Diego, California, 2016

For the next 12 years, I tried virtually everything to get me back to "normal"—everything but SSRIs. The idea of popping pills to fix a symptom instead of addressing the underlying issue seemed careless. You could say I had a bias against Western medicine. In high school, I read *Spontaneous Healing* by Dr. Andrew Weil, which had a profound impact on my life. It taught me how intelligent our bodies are and how physical, spiritual, and mental health were intertwined. In a way, this book planted a seed of mistrust in Western/allopathic medicine.

I had also grown up with the influences of traditional *hanbang*, Korean Oriental medicine. As a form of colonial resistance, thousands of

Korean physicians in the 1930s organized conferences, research, and findings that refuted Japan's stance that Western medicine was superior. It had been *hanbang* that had saved thousands of lives in rural Korea, as medical facilities had been sparse and inaccessible for so many. Japanese colonial rule had tried to eradicate Korean medicine, but the *hanbang* traditions remained pervasive in Korean households, including ours.

Hanbang wasn't some superstitious or charlatan practice. My father, who has a background in pharmacology and used to own a pharmacy, often turned to *hanbang*. When my sister was having health issues, my parents drove her two hours to see a *hanuisa*, a Korean Oriental doctor. My mother would then prepare the herbal remedies for my sister. The pungent smell of herbs would fill the entire house as my mother boiled large batches of the herbal tonics the *hanuisa* had prescribed. I, too, went to a hanuisa for my health issues and drank the bitter herbal tonics. I had even witnessed my father practice bloodletting, a practice used to balance ki (the Korean pronunciation of chi, energy), on a sick man rather than recommending any kind of pharma meds. That's not to say that my father never recommended drugs. He just turned to them as a last resort. So you can imagine my reluctance to take pharmaceuticals.

After my divorce, I enrolled in a yoga teacher training course and spent the next several years of my life immersed in the health and wellness community. I helped launch San Diego's largest yoga wellness center, managing a staff of 30, while running and operating a weekly schedule of 180 classes. Alternative healing was my entire world.

During my tenure at the yoga center, I experimented with various healing modalities, with practitioners who swore they could help me. *You just need to practice ABC more or stop doing XYZ. Have you tried this protocol? Or what about this oil? Try this past life regression. I swear it heals everything.* In between long runs on the beach, plus all of the above, I immersed myself in reading books on self-improvement, psychology, spirituality, and going to therapy. Yet, my eating disorder worsened, and the depressive episodes kept me in a loop of self-loathing and exhaustion.

How was I still so broken when I'd done nearly everything to fix myself? What the fuck was I doing wrong? Was I not eating right? Did I have demons inside of me? What unresolved issues did I have that I needed to talk out further? What inner child work did I need to do? Which shaman should I go to next? It became a never-ending search.

Drastic diet changes, meditation practices, yoga, self-help books, seminars, running, microdosing with psychedelics, past life regression, waking up at 6 a.m., marijuana, positive psychology, talk therapy, hypnosis, spiritual exorcisms, Traditional Chinese Medicine, reiki, church, gratitude journals, minimalist living, walking, extended periods in nature, chiropractic visits, homeopathy, MDMA, silent retreats, and so many other paths to get out of depression.

I kept telling myself that I just needed to get my shit together. *Be more positive. Write more in your gratitude journal. Exercise more. Eat better. Meditate more.* After twelve years of trying to do more, I realized I had no more in me. My friend Dala, who is a trusted friend with a

Ph.D. in psychology, gave me the number of a practitioner who specialized in depression. A few weeks later, I found myself sitting in Columbia University's Psychiatry waiting room. I felt like one big contradiction, a weak-minded hypocrite for trying to solve my problems with a pill. But more than a decade had gone by since I had my first depressive episode, and I was barely hanging on. At the height of it all, I sat in the bathroom with a razor in hand, crying in desperation for the misery to go away. But I knew I hadn't exhausted *all* my options. There was still psychiatry. *Go to the psychiatrist. What have you got to lose? You've already hit rock bottom.*

A therapeutic dose of Lexapro starts anywhere from 10-20mg, but my doctor started me on a microdose of 2.5 mg to ease my apprehension about introducing pills into my body. Even with this small dose, I started to notice micro changes. It wasn't so difficult to wake up. A few weeks later my dosage went up to 5 mg—still a microdose. Not long after that, leaving my house got easier, and basic tasks, including brushing my teeth and showering, no longer felt like mountains to climb. Ruminations of suicide tapered. Around the same time, I began seeing a psychologist. With a psychiatrist in one hand and a psychologist in the other, my walk to recovery began picking up. A few months later, I was practicing yoga five days a week.

In less than a year, I was more alive and active. My anxiety went down, and my sense of confusion and despair no longer interfered with my day-to-day well-being. With self-care rituals in place, work expanding, and my social life going rather well, I felt ready to transition away from the SSRIs. But, not long after I began tapering off my meds, things quickly unraveled. I locked myself up in my apartment, not leaving for days, afraid of what the outside world would bring.

SoHo, New York, 2015

After several months of uncontrolled spiraling, I decided to go back on the meds. My doctor increased the dose to 10 mg. Within a few weeks, the suicidal thoughts waned, and my fear of leaving my apartment subsided. Things started stabilizing again, and after six months passed, I wanted off the meds again. I didn't like that I had grown "dependent" on these meds.

In the "conscious" community, allopathic pharmacology is viewed with skepticism. When I shared my challenges with depression, I received tons of unsolicited advice from folks, including those who had never even had depression. *Have you tried sitting in ceremony? You do realize that you're just taking a placebo pill, right? Let me recommend this supplement for you. It helps with serotonin production. Oh, you're playing into the big pharma matrix. You're avoiding the real work by taking drugs.* Everyone seemed to have an opinion about my health, and in part, I agreed with them. Each time I took my meds, I judged myself for lacking spiritual strength.

This time, I would taper off my meds with microdosing with psilocybin. I had done a great deal of research on psychedelic-assisted therapies and had shared my plan with a progressive doctor I had been seeing. She supported my decision and would assist me throughout the process.

***

Three months after tapering with microdosing, the ground began to slip out from underneath me once again. All the healthy habits and rituals I had built fell by the wayside. My recurring dreams during this time were about swimming against a current and feeling exhausted and barely being able to keep my head above water. Worries about keeping my business afloat kept me awake at night. I questioned my self-worth, and whether I deserved to live. But I didn't seem to have the strength to keep swimming against what felt like a current that wanted to carry me away under the waves, never to re-emerge. If I can't fulfill my dreams, then I'm a fraud, and if I'm a fraud, then I'm no one. I'm over thirty and have been searching for three decades to find some peace, and if I'm not going to find it now, then maybe I ought to give up looking for it.

With bills piling up and not knowing when my next client was coming, I resorted to the only thing that I knew I could control. My eating disorder went back in full swing. The cookie monster inside promised to take the bitterness out of life with sweet sugar rushes, only to crash an hour later. But I'd prove to the cookie monster who was stronger by starving myself for a few days. Since I had vindicated myself, I could reward myself with pints of Ben and Jerry's ice cream, but my lactose intolerance would scold me, and I'd starve myself again. As punishment, I would not leave my apartment for days at a time. Ashamed I could not control myself, I resigned that I was unfit for society. Who could love or want this worthless piece of shit as a friend when I had nothing but an empty cup of desperation and a suitcase full of self-pity? Another sun set and another moon rose. I longed for the dark to stay. At times, my apartment felt more like solitary confinement than home.

Why are you making things so difficult for yourself? Why not just go back on the meds? I asked myself. That damn Catholic conditioning, though. The angel on my shoulder would say, *Of course, it's painful. This is the path to the kingdom. No pain, no gain. Even the Buddha starved himself.*

I called Desiree, who had experience with mental illness and medication. Years ago, she had been beaten into submission by the police and then handcuffed to a hospital bed during her first manic episode. But having bipolar did not handicap her. Desiree is a Traditional Chinese Medicine (TCM) doctor and acupuncturist, who has helped thousands heal their physical illnesses, from cancer to diabetes, and spiritual challenges from worthiness to purpose. To manage her bipolar, she uses TCM and allopathic medicine. Despite all the stigma and poor mental healthcare in the U.S., Desiree has become the mother of three healthy children, the CEO of her own multi-million-dollar business, and one of the most generous humans I know. I've never heard her judge herself, or anyone for that matter, for taking meds.

I asked her, "Given the work you do, how is it that you're not off of your medication?"

She said, "No one said that Western medicine doesn't have a place or a value in healing. Depending on your ailment, you need a different tool. And thankfully, because of my medication, I have been able to thrive."

A hammer is a mighty tool, but it's not the best tool for screwing things into the wall. Soon after I spoke to Desiree, I wrote to Erica, my friend who is a nurse practitioner *and* naturopath. We decided, after taking inventory of my well-being over the last three months, that I would start taking Lexapro again. A wave of judgment came and went away immediately. I decided not to spend my energy comparing my health decisions with others', but focus on getting better.

Several weeks later, I began to see improvements in my behavior. Over time I stabilized, and I have continued to take my meds uninterrupted for several years now. Let me be clear, the pill alone did not solve all my problems. I continued going to therapy and had a team of healthcare practitioners with whom I consistently met. I continued to diligently take care of myself and complement my meds with meditation, diet, and lifestyle changes, along with alternative therapies. Taking a page out of my father, Desiree, and Erica's books, I used Eastern and Western practices. Like the rest of my journey in life, learning how to care for myself has been an experiment—trial and error.

Taking pills did not fix the relapses that I would have with self-doubt, self-worth, and self-acceptance. No pill can do that. However, my medication did help me stabilize enough so that I could stop the treadmill of suicidal ideation. With medication, I could tread water just enough to keep swimming and not sink. I still have challenging periods, but I am happy to say that I have not seen the cookie monster in a few years. When I don't want to leave the house or talk to people, I have a greater self-understanding that withdrawing from the outside world is a part of my process. The seasons when I'm mercurial and dark no longer hold the same power over me as they once did. Pema Chödrön writes:

> *"Having compassion starts and ends with having compassion for all those unwanted parts of ourselves. The healing comes from letting there be room for all of this to happen: room for grief, for relief, for misery, for joy."*

Over the next two years, I developed greater self-acceptance. I now had more than a hammer in my toolbox; I had my rituals and meds to support me. That didn't make me weak; it made me handier. It broadened my perspective and allowed me to embrace the work in progress called life.

A while ago my brother, who views therapy and mental health with snake-oil skepticism said to me, "You're on anti-despressants? I can't believe you're taking those. Do you even know how bad those are for you? You shouldn't be taking them."

My response—a silent smile. It doesn't matter what my brother or anyone else thinks about my health or life. I am the sole caretaker of this body, and I choose life.

To those of you suffering from depression, asking for support is not a sign of weakness. It is a sign of courage and hope.

Photo of me, taken by Ziad Zaatari in Sayda, Lebanon, 2017

13

ROSE QUARTZ

I hadn't seen Kimi in nearly a year when she invited me to come to her new digs in Austin. The two of us had both relocated to Austin right before the pandemic, leaving New York for something slower and more spacious. I wasn't sure if I was at the right door, but after knocking and waiting, I checked to see if the front door was unlocked. Five feet into the empty house I saw a red neon sign, "Pleasure Room," lighting the all-black furnished room. There was a canopy bed with black sheets and a St. Andrew's cross, a bondage installation. Yes. I was definitely in the right place.

"Just got your text. But I see you got in," Kimi said as I was still looking at her pleasure room.

"Love the setup, babe," I purred.

"Right? It's where we were doing workshops. Now with the pan-

[111]

demic, though, it's just one-on-one client sessions that I do in there."

Kimi is a somatic and conscious kink therapist. As a somatic therapist, she uses kink and pleasure to help clients explore various challenges. I knew she was a dominatrix but had never seen her home office. I was curious about the room, and luckily I wasn't the only one. Another guest asked, "Can you give us a tour of the pleasure room?"

"Of course."

What I found more intriguing than the St. Andrew's cross installation was her perfectly organized drawers of toys and tools.

"Would you like to do a little play?"

"*Hell yes!*"

"Well, the first thing I like to introduce to clients is some spanking. Would you guys like to start with that?"

"Sure!"

"There are many erogenous zones on the human body, and the buttocks being quite close to the genitals heightens the blood flow to the erotic zone of the genitals. Before making any contact, though, the dom and sub should communicate with each other. (Oh, and for those in the room who don't know, dom and sub are short for dominatrix and submissive). Verbal and non-verbal communication is key. We usually start by communicating our boundaries and levels of comfort. I like to use a simple scale from 1-10. All my first-time client sessions will go only to a seven. This way we're always maintaining a safe connection. So who'd like to go first?"

"Sign me up!" said one of her friends, and we all giggled like naughty schoolchildren.

Kimi had her friend come up to the St. Andrew's cross, and her partner Jesse began buckling the cuffs around her wrists.

She continued, "Now there are different ways of spanking. Here's how you shape your hand." She showed us the differences between a flat-shaped hand versus a slightly round shape. "You'll notice the difference in sound. You hear?"

The room was silent with concentration. It was like we were in a university lecture hall.

"You can also play with tempo." She demonstrated on her eager volunteer.

I had no idea there was such an art to all of it. This practice requires a great deal of listening and mindfulness, attuning to your partner's breathing and body language. It's like a dance of sorts.

After everyone else had gone, Kimi turned to me and asked, "Do you want to try?"

"Yes," I smiled.

I walked to the cross, and Jesse cuffed me. I could feel my heart beating. My body, without any spanking, was already coming alive. I immediately became alert. As Kimi began petting my butt, I softened a bit, and then she gave me a little tap on the butt.

She asked me on a scale from 1-10 what level that was for me.

One.

She struck my butt again but with a bit more force.

Two.

She continued to develop a bit more speed and force.

Four.

She asked if I wanted to continue.

Yes.

The progression of slaps continued with greater force, and I was slowly moving from *four* to *five* to *six*. She increased the speed and intensity, asking me how I was doing.

Six. I knew that there was still much more to explore with intensity and that I was nowhere near my discomfort yet, but since we were doing an intro Kimi suggested Jesse uncuff me.

After I was released, I playfully walked over to the bed and leaned over on the side, taunting her to be smacked.

"Oh, does someone want more?" Kimi asked.

"I want to see what an *eight* feels like."

We went from a *four* to an *eight* with ease, and when I felt the eight, I told Kimi. Even though I knew I could have continued, I decided to wait. Something in me told me to go slow. So we stopped there at an *eight*. I touched my butt, and it was warm. So much blood had rushed there. Was I aroused? Yes. But not in the "ravish me" kind of way. It was an arousal of senses, a heightened awareness of my surroundings. I was out of my head and in my body. It was very evident that this conscious kink had somatic powers.

***

Three weeks later, Kimi threw a naughty secret Santa holiday party. In the mix of the Secret Santa gifts were mini vibrators, bondage kits, non-toxic lube, hero costumes, and various adult card games.

I recognized four other people at the party, but the rest of the cast that night was new to me. This was a room full of characters, Austin style. They don't say "keep Austin weird" for nothing. But weird is my speed; it's one of the reasons I loved New York.

One person in the crowd stood out to me. He resembled a younger, better-looking version of Hulk Hogan. His astro-Viking Burning Man outfit fit like a glove, wearing a leopard print onesie, with metallic cape and all. As I admired his get-up, a woman came and sat on his lap. He held her tenderly. The Viking's softness warmed my heart from across the room. In my own experience and Hollywood-imprinted mind, I had never seen a man of the Rock's stature display such tenderness.

Later that evening, I had a conversation with him in the kitchen and discovered that he was a professional MMA fighter and had an organization that helps bring clean water to vulnerable communities abroad. He was in Austin to record a podcast show with his buddy Joe Rogan. The MMA fighters I knew included my ex-husband and his circle of friends, who were all far from tender.

As the party continued, the Viking and his partner asked about the pleasure room. By this hour, the group had dwindled to about seven of us. Kimi began her introduction of spanking and walked each person through it. I watched as Jesse cuffed the Viking's partner, and the Viking moved behind the cross so that the two would be face to face. As Kimi spanked the Viking's partner, the Viking began petting her head and whispering to her. With each strike, their breaths synchronized deeper and more intensely. If Mary had been the one hanging, this is how I imagine Jesus would have supported her from behind. I was seeing the Ecstasy of Saint Teresa right before me.

When they finished, I looked Kimi in the eyes and said, "I want to let go tonight." Her simple nod told me she knew what I meant. As Jesse cuffed me, Kimi reminded me to breathe. Just hanging there, I could already feel my body become more alive. The rest of the world melted away, and now it was just the three of us—Kimi behind me and Jesse in front of me. I wasn't sure I wanted his support. Could I trust this man to hold space for me? Was I sending the wrong message and inviting sexual advances? My mind was going a mile a minute, but Jesse knew what to say: "Breathe."

Kimi immediately began at a *five*. My blood was already simmering with heat. Why was I already so worked up this early on? Was I extra tense with anticipation? Or was this all part of the experience? Then on the next strike, I heard a wail. It was my voice. Another strike, another wail. As the tempo and intensity picked up, there were no more questions, no thinking, just breathing and moaning. Growls came out of me that I never knew I had. Even through my yells, I could hear Jesse whisper, "Breathe. Let go."

That's when I lost all self-consciousness about others being in the house. I didn't care if I woke up the entire neighborhood. Between the unpredictable pattern of Kimi's strikes, I could feel my nerves turn to anger, my blood accelerating from simmer to boiling, making each strike more intense and the yells louder. Tears started spilling out. It wasn't the physical pain that made me scream; it was something deeper. Kimi asked me if I still wanted to continue. "Yes. I'm ready to let it all go."

As the intensity grew, I pressed my head into Jesse's chest, breathing, crying, and screaming all at once. In the cavity of his chest, between strikes, I told myself, "Don't try to anticipate the next strike. Be present."

And in those subsequent strikes, the kettle inside screamed.

I knew others were watching, but I didn't care who was in the room at that point anymore. Kimi asked how I was doing, and I said, "Keep going."

I screamed all the pain I had experienced. Pain that was stored in my body that had been trapped inside for so many years. All my fears around my identity, body, work, everything. It was all out for the entire world to hear.

Then she paused.

After a bit of silence, I told her, "I'm finished."

As Jesse uncuffed me, I was dizzy, in a trance of sorts. I had gone somewhere beyond the cellular level of my body. Kimi and Jesse helped me walk to the bed and cradled me.

"You are safe. You are safe," Kimi whispered, rocking me back and forth. And as I breathed deeply, a calm overcame me. "You are safe," I repeated. There, cradled between Kimi and Jesse, I saw what intimacy could look like. It didn't have to be domineering or submissive as I had witnessed throughout my life. This was whole. Unity of yin and yang.

Still in my cocoon, the Viking and his partner came to say goodbye. The Viking looked at me and said, "It was an honor to be able to witness you surrender like that." He had seen me.

Kimi and Jesse walked me upstairs to their guest bedroom and tucked me in bed. That night, I slept like a baby.

***

A week later, I got a text from Kimi inviting me to a gathering where we would set intentions for the winter solstice. The Viking and his partner were there. Strangers no more, we hugged as kindred spirits. In the crowd, though, there were others who I did not know. One had a shaved head with tats all over his body; the other was a zebra rancher with a larger-than-life stature. There was also an intimidating gay man whom I had met at the Santa party. I think there were more men than women in the room. My anxiety meter rose. Not sure if I'll be able to open up and share at this gathering in front of these men, but here goes.

The gathering was facilitated by Dennis, who guides authentic communication through qi gong and movement integration. He asked us to take up space and find a comfortable place to start. I decided to go into the other room, where I would be somewhat alone and not near the intimidating men.

One of the first exercises was to dance with one another. In that dance, I avoided all the men. I didn't want to risk being looked at in a sexually predatory way as I had been conditioned to think all men do. My Catholic mother, movies, porn, etc. had all taught me that men were after only one thing with women—to use you for sex. Conditioning had told me that it was my responsibility as a woman to avoid precarious situations that would invite unwelcome advances; otherwise, it was just asking for it. But I remembered a conversation I had with my sister about unfreezing my heart. If I ever wanted to be in another relationship, I would have to learn to trust men again. That evening, I decided to test the waters.

During the second exercise of the evening, I slowly made my way toward the men and danced alongside them. Instead of fear, I decided to dance as though I was in the room with people I loved. My reptilian brain was no longer scanning the room for predators. For the first time, I forgot about the male gaze and danced without care.

At the end of the evening, we gathered in a circle to share our experiences. The Viking eagerly started. In his story, he shared how he had battled drug abuse. One night, after a long bender of a party, he made up his mind to commit suicide. He went down to the beach with a bunch of pills in hand, ready to end his life with an overdose and drown himself in the ocean. But as the sun rose, the beauty of the ocean overwhelmed him, and he released the pills into the water. Then the rancher spoke, and he shared grievances that he had been dealing with in his family, which were deeply painful. As I heard their stories, I saw a bit of myself in them. I, too, had struggled with family, and I, too, had contemplated ending it all.

As the shares were coming to completion and the circle was about to close, my hand rose. I nervously shared, "For years I've been afraid to trust men. I've been scared that a man would try to abuse me or control me. But I don't want to let this fear run my life anymore. When Dennis asked us to dance with one another, I initially avoided the men in this room. It's what makes me feel in control. But for some reason, I felt safe not doing that tonight. I want to thank all the men in this room for helping me feel safe and overcome this fear." When I finished, I looked at the Viking and Jesse and smiled.

Silence filled the room. Then the Viking spoke. "Can I say one thing? I'd like to gift you something. When I was going through this difficult time, I bought this crystal. I'm sorry you've experienced that pain. On behalf of the men in this room—I hope it's okay to include the men here—I'd like to give you this rose quartz. May it make you feel safe, as it has for me." In front of all the men and women in the room, he handed me a beautiful rose quartz medallion, and we embraced each other in the middle of the circle.

After the circle closed, the rancher came up to me and said, "Thank you for sharing what you shared. It meant a lot." Then the tattooed man and I struck up a conversation, and I discovered that he had a men's circle helping others to heal the masculine. There I was, surrounded by men who were healing just as I was healing.

Right after that, I went out with the men and decided to have a smoke of tobacco to end the night ceremoniously. I started feeling sick. Surely, it could not have been the tobacco.

But after a few puffs, I began to recognize the nausea I was feeling. It was the kind I felt when I was a little girl, scared to visit my sister who had been disowned, not knowing what my father would do if he found out. I made a quick and graceful exit, hugging each of the men, and walked quickly to my car. As I drove off, the intensity of the nausea grew stronger. I couldn't hold this down anymore. I pulled over, opened the car door, and began purging. What I purged was not food, but all the toxicity that I had consumed, the accumulation of fears fed one generation after another.

As I wiped my mouth, a smile came across my face. I can trust men. I let go of the toxic feminine and masculine that was inside of me. Between the screaming the weekend prior and this evening's ceremony, my body finally let go. Not only could I trust men, but I could also trust myself.

Winter Solstice, New York, 2018

14

EVERYWHERE BUT ELSEWHERE

When I was a little girl, my father asked me what I wanted to be when I grew up. If not a Broadway singer or costume designer, I'd almost always say flight attendant. At an early age, I already knew *elsewhere* was the destination.

On the drive to the airport, as my father is screaming at my mother, wondering how stupid she could be for having forgotten to pack his who-remembers-what, I feel utter shame in the backseat. Could people on the road see what my father saw in us— how useless we were or how much of an "animal" my mother was, as my father used to call her? It wasn't enough that my mother had packed everything else for the family trip—down to the safety pins required to make my father's makeshift traditional Korean-style travel pillow. When we got to the airport, my father opened the trunk, pulled out our suitcases, and dumped everything on the ground. My favorite stuffed animal, books, and crayons fell to the ground, scattered beside my mother's clothing and makeup.

I didn't want to get on that flight, but I had no other choice. Seven years old was too early for emancipation.

Since leaving for university at 17, I have moved nearly every year. I moved from one lease to the next, never staying in one place for longer than a year. The moment I left home for university, I vowed never to live under the control of my parents again. I searched for what would be home in every place I moved.

That's probably why two years fresh out of university, I got married. The problem, though, is that I didn't know what a functional home looked like.

Leaving my husband in the middle of the day while he was at work set the precedent for how fast I could pack and how little I needed to take with me to get the hell out. *Fight or flight?* asked my reptilian brain. *Flight*, of course. And when the plane took off, I felt a wave of calm wash over me. Soaring above the clouds, I was safe. No one could touch me here.

***

Above the Clouds, Heading to Turkey, 2017

After separating, I moved back to San Diego and lived with my sister. That only lasted for a few months before she moved to Costa Rica.

[125]

Now homeless with one sister out of the picture, I didn't know where I'd go. That's when Desiree, my best friend from high school, asked me for the hundredth time, "Why don't you move in with me? C'mon. It'll be fun."

At 23, she already had her own home, while I was barely making rent and paying for gas with all my part-time jobs, which included tutoring, teaching voice lessons, being a personal trainer at L.A. Fitness, and getting my benefits as a barista at Starbucks. I remember writing emails to my ex's lawyer in the Starbucks parking lot during breaks. Since I couldn't afford to hire a lawyer, I represented myself.

Even when I was under financial stress and exhausted from driving from one job to the next, I remembered my mother's words to me, "Don't take his money. Build yourself back up on your own." That's when I decided I would only ask for compensation to go to counseling. At the time, I was paying $50 per therapy session. When I received his lawyer's email stating her client was unwilling to cover my therapy, I wrote back, "He can either pay for two years of therapy, or he can give me what I am legally entitled to, including alimony, 50% of the trust, houses, bank accounts, cars, etc. Also, please remind your client that I will file a harassment suit if he ever contacts me again."

The text and phone call threats from my ex ceased immediately, and a week later, the divorce papers were signed. I got exactly what I asked for: two years' worth of therapy paid and an agreement that he would never contact me or approach my family or me again. When I found out my divorce was finalized, Desiree and I went to our usual joint to celebrate. The Golden Spoon—the best frozen yogurt.

I can't tell you how many calories we spent on frozen yogurt, talking about life, relationships, our dreams, and pains.

As I was about to head over to my parents' house for Easter with my family, I got a phone call from my mother. "Everyone thinks you're still married and living in Washington D.C. People will wonder why you've come to church without your husband. Maybe it's best you not come to church with us. Sorry." Under any other circumstance, I would have been relieved not to have to sit through church with my parents, but instead, I was venting over froyo with Desiree. *Geezus!* The hypocrisy of it all.

***

About a year and a half later, Desiree had a whirlwind of a romance and got married within two months of meeting her husband. Once again, it was time for me to pack up and find a new home.

Like an orphan, I moved in with my brother and his family. At 25, I was sleeping on the top bunk with my nine-year-old niece and her dog, Autumn, on the bottom. The stitches Desiree had helped me sew after my divorce quickly cut open while living with my brother. His passive-aggressive jokes jabbed at my tender wounds. I knew he cared deep down, but I felt so unwanted in his home. It hurt when he'd call me a child in front of my niece and nephew. I was doing my damnedest to get my life back on track, working multiple jobs and being responsible. All I ever wanted was some acknowledgment and encouragement that everything would be okay.

Feeling as though I didn't belong anywhere, I made the decision to travel to India and spend some time in an ashram. Perhaps some meditation could help me find my purpose. Even though I could have asked my parents for financial support, I didn't want to be at the mercy of my father's moods. If the wind blew the wrong way, my father could cut you off. I was through with men trying to control my life. Freedom became my obsession.

A few weeks before my departure, a yoga teacher of mine asked if I'd cancel my trip to manage the yoga center she had just opened. After a few days of thinking over her offer, I accepted.

I found a room to rent in a place two blocks from the ocean. It would be less than a five-minute drive to the yoga center. Living there on Bonair Street in Windansea, La Jolla would be the longest I'd stay in one place—nearly two years. It was enough time to try out "steady life." I stopped working five jobs and focused on one. My steady boyfriend at the time had been in the same 9-to-5, lived in the same apartment, and had the same routines for years. And while it seemed appealing to be with someone who "had their shit together," I felt like I was missing out on life. Steady was vanilla.

If there was one flavor Des and I never got at The Golden Spoon, it was vanilla. Who gets vanilla when there are so many other flavors?

I concluded that being in relationships did not mesh well with my desire to be free. What did give me a sense of freedom, though, was work. My career became my obsession. Making money and supporting myself filled a longing in my heart to be free—to leave whenever I wanted, whether from a raging father or a controlling husband. I figured the more money I had, the faster I could escape these ghosts.

That's when I decided to go to grad school and get my M.B.A. in Finance—the ultimate ticket to freedom—or so I thought. Instead, it got me golden handcuffs. The space above the clouds that had once been my sanctuary soon turned into a grind. Monday through Thursday, I traveled for work, and on nearly every flight, I had my laptop out, only to get in the cab to continue working on my phone and then get to the hotel and open my laptop again. After a year on this hamster wheel, I concluded that freedom would not be found under the auspices of working for the man.

Off to find freedom again, I traveled around the world for the next five years, moving coast to coast, country to country, city to city. My newly chosen vocation as a photographer made me hungry to search for story after story, photograph after photograph. My brother asked, 'All this traveling seems like you're either running away from something or searching for something. Which is it?"

Both. Is that not the tension required for a great story?

***

January 2020 came, and I was feeling exhausted from life. I needed a break. Desiree invited me to visit her in Austin. I found the city underwhelming with little cultural diversity, but New York and all my other travels since quitting my job had overwhelmed my nervous system. Maybe underwhelm would be good for my adrenal fatigue. That visit with Des planted a seed: maybe I could start growing some roots in Austin. Just maybe, I could finally settle down.

A few weeks later, I flew to New York. I made up my mind that I would wrap up my remaining projects in New York and move to Austin. A few days before a final client shoot, I got a phone call from my client. It was Thursday, March 12, 2020. "It looks like we're going to close our doors for the foreseeable future." By the hour, the situation in New York was growing more serious. It would only be a matter of days before the lockdowns in Italy would spread to New York. I knew I had to get out as soon as possible. There was no way I'd survive trapped in an apartment in New York.

Immediately after I got off the phone with my client, I booked a one-way ticket to Austin.

"Des, can I stay with you?"

"Yep. What time is your flight? I'll come get you."

I left New York on Friday the 13th, March 2020.

**

The first few weeks after landing in Austin, I slept. While the whole world panicked about the uncertainty of their futures, jobs, housing situation, finances, and separation from loved ones, and with everything around them going up in flames, I finally got the permission I needed to rest. That whole "what am I going to do now?" anxiety that swept the entire world—I had that down to a *T*. I was all too familiar with the blazing Tower tarot card. The imagery shows people jumping out of a tower set ablaze by a fierce fire-breathing dragon.

The pandemonium of fire, dragon, and falling people distracts people from seeing the small white dove at the top. The dove symbolizes that a calm will come after a storm. Fire purifies and transforms; it is the only element that cannot be polluted. What is no longer serving you—the skyscrapers, the ego, climbing higher—burns away. Instead of jumping out of the tower, I dreamt of the dove. If there's one thing I learned through all the uncertainty in my life, it's that we'd survive. *This too shall pass.*

After a few weeks of deep rest, I re-emerged to find myself surrounded by a sea of people looking for a life jacket. The Great Resignation had washed over the entire country, and more than ever, people were starting to ask the tough questions that I had been asking myself since the day I left my marriage at 23, and again at 32 when I quit my job. *What do you do when there's no roadmap for where you're going, and it's dark as fuck?* I didn't want anyone to go through what I had gone through alone, as I had in those arduous years. If I could help just one other person keep at it for even one more day, then I would know my choices had not been in vain. With lockdowns and no way to photograph others, I decided to turn the camera around on myself and started sharing what I knew best: how to reinvent yourself with whatever you've got.

On April 2, 2020, I taught my first workshop ever, titled *Your Badass Bio*. The purpose of the workshop was to help people tap back into their ikigai, the Japanese term for "reason for being," and write a bio that would help each participant remember how badass they are. So badass that they could start that business they'd always dreamed of or apply for another job between furloughs and layoffs. If I could go from being a failed opera singer and post-bacc pre-med dropout to Starbucks barista to yogi-entrepreneur to recovering Fortune 500 management consultant to photographer, writer, and business coach, then anyone else could reinvent themselves too. It's not because I was lucky or had some special sauce. If you saw my human design, numerology, or astrology charts, you probably wouldn't want my life. I was destined to say Yes to It All, even if it meant years of trial and error. Six weeks after that initial workshop, I was teaching to a ZOOM room with over 500 attendees.

In a matter of weeks, I went from photographer to business coach, and in the fall of 2020, I co-founded a support group for women entrepreneurs called A Creative Mastermind. That summer, I produced and hosted my first online summit called Permission to Promote, aimed at getting people to overcome their fear of putting their work out into the world. I also began writing this book. In a single quarter, I made nearly as much as I had the year prior. Perhaps traveling had been a distraction all these years, I thought. Maybe my flight phase was over, and I could finally settle down.

But one afternoon, as I was sitting on the back porch writing the outline of this book, the wind caught my attention. "*Go,*" it whispered through the leaves. At first, I thought this was my mind playing tricks on me to avoid writing. But the wind blew harder, "It's time to leave. Go to Tulum." *Move? Really?* Just when I was starting to get comfortable in Austin.

After checking into my accommodations in Tulum, I discovered that my Airbnb was on a street called Kulkukan—the Mayan deity of the winds.

2020 was supposed to be the year I would go to Mongolia. My dear friend Jeff and I were planning a photography adventure trip. He had put together an itinerary where we would travel through Mongolia, and I would show others how to see another world through a lens. It had always been a dream of mine to travel to Mongolia. That's where Eve Arnold made so many of her beautiful photos, especially the ones of horses. I imagined that the heart of these photos was coming from a place of freedom. The Mongols are one of the last remaining nomadic cultures on the planet, and I admired this way of living, for they are a part of my ancestry, my lineage. My father used to call me a wild horse—telling me I would gallop about with free rein. I longed to experience the spirit of unbridled freedom. For so long, there had been a bit placed in my mouth, forcing me to keep it shut on all my desires.

But instead of flying east to meet the horse's call, I'd go south to Mexico.

The first night I got into Tulum, my friend Elsa messaged me: "Welcome! There's a dinner happening at a friend's house. Come over."

While sitting on the couch, connecting with new friends in Tulum, the subject of horses came up. "My friend David is going to do a horse constellation next week. Do you want to come?"

"What? There are horse constellations in Tulum? I have to meet this guy."

Horses in Tulum are uncommon due to a specific fly that causes them to get sick. David explained to me, though, that he was able to

[133]

find a horse ranch in Cancun. I had done a horse constellation a year prior facilitated by my friend Matisse, and it unlocked hidden stories in my ancestry. I met my grandmother for the first time. She had already passed before I was born. But there, I could see her suffering. The resentment that I had been carrying toward the #youtoo'ers had been her anger that had been passed down to me. "Do what you have to do. Suck it up. You're not special. This is survival, and you do whatever you have to do. That doesn't mean you get a red carpet roll-out."

Traditional family constellations, developed by German psychotherapist Bert Hellinger, draws from Gestalt therapy, psychoanalysis, and Zulu traditions. Think psychology meets ancient animistic tradition in a therapeutic practice to help understand family dynamics. Coupling family constellations with horses, this practice reveals systemic family dynamics through the observation of these highly sensitive creatures.

Horses have an electromagnetic field five times greater than that of humans. In fact, their survival depends on their heightened sensitivity to their environment. Moreover, like dogs, horses have cohabited with humans for thousands of years. Without horses, we would not have been able to travel and build empires or massive civilizations. Horses know humans well. It's not every day an opportunity to do a horse constellation comes along, no less in the Yucatan.

***

We're nearing the end of the horse constellation, and all three horses have moved into the small rectangular enclosure, away from the much bigger circular enclosure.

David asks me, "So what do you want to do now?"

"Let's move her back into the circular enclosure and see what happens," I suggest. I walk over to the horse that represents me in this constellation and guide her to the round enclosure. As soon as I release the reins, she turns and walks back into the rectangular enclosure.

"What do you make of this? Is it possible she prefers it in there?" David asks as I'm standing in the circle alone.

"I don't want to be in the rectangle, though."

"Why not?"

I'm not sure how to respond.

Squares are worse than vanilla. From the moment we're born, we're asked to fit into squares. Our birth certificate requires us to fit into boxes: gender, race of father, race of mother, occupation of father, occupation of mother, and so on.

Throughout our lives, we're put into more boxes, beginning early on with aptitude tests and scores that determine a child's intelligence. Children who are far too intelligent and have higher skills beyond memorization and spitting facts are told to behave, sit still, and keep their mouths. They're forced into a curriculum that is no more than an assembly line for bots.

Our self-expression these days is limited to more boxes: swipe left, swipe right, and in our About sections on LinkedIn we try to cram as much of our lives into one tiny box as possible, so we can check more boxes.

You know who also loved boxes? Hitler.

[x] Blond

[x] Blue eyes

[x] Straight

[ ] No illnesses

If you check the wrong box, you can be sure some Trump will deport your ass and separate you from your children.

I grew up in one of the biggest squares ever—the suburban strip mall. My parents owned several dry cleaners, each in a strip mall with a fast food chain across the street, a bank, a grocery store, a nail salon, a pizza joint, a local bar, a liquor store, a laundromat, and a wretched asphalt parking lock outlined with white cells. I spent my childhood in strip malls, and only had my imagination, books, and writing to escape from the doldrum of this prison. When my friends went to hang out, I couldn't go because I had no ride. My mother would be too busy working, and my father would be out golfing. So the strip mall became my playground. On the off chance I got a ride, I couldn't enjoy my time with friends. I'd be too distracted by the dread of returning to the square I hated the most—home. I felt trapped there. My sisters and brother were much older than me, so I grew up alone in a home where I witnessed my parents fighting and had to fend for myself against these other inmates. I just wanted out as fast as I could. Like a bee that accidentally flies into a car, I darted madly from window to window, trying to find an escape.

When I see the horse back in the rectangular enclosure, I let out, "I just don't. I don't like squares. I *hate* squares. I'd rather be in the circle."

David responds with, "Careful not to be a slave to freedom."

I've been moving from country to country, city to city, job to job, searching for the nearest exit. At the first sign of entrapment, I flee, for better or worse. But the greatest entrapment was the wall I had built up around my heart. Never go deep unless you want to get your heart broken and end up in a prison of a marriage like your mother or working in a strip mall. My restlessness to escape had become my prison. The frontier I searched for madly like a busy bee was not outside. Through the pandemic and global lockdown, I discovered what true freedom meant. It was finding stillness as I traveled to the place most distant from me all this time—my heart. Everywhere but elsewhere.

Here.

Portrait by Renato . Sian Ka'an, Tulum, Mexico, 2021

15

PASSING OF AUTUMN

Autumn is a rescue dog. She has the jump of a Jack Russell terrier, the ears of a hound, a longish body resembling a dachshund's, and short smooth hair, the color of a buttery croissant. Her greeting is a trampoline pounce to your belly, one jump after another in an attempt to hug you.

Even when there are others in the house, Autumn stays glued to my niece's hip. The two dream together, but when my niece leaves for school she switches beds and dreams with my brother, the boss. She knows who else loves her almost as much as my niece does. I wish she'd cuddle with me when I'm working in the living room. But even Autumn knows I am the weird homeless aunt who's overstayed her welcome.

My niece trains Autumn how to sit, lie down, and shake hands.

This communication between the two is one of the rare moments when I get to see my niece smile. In fact, she's smiling and interacting with the family more since Autumn entered the picture. We used to confuse her silence with moodiness because we are Korean, and Koreans are anything but quiet. Our politicians are notorious for breaking out into brawls during congressional sessions, and our spicy kimchi and chili paste add to our fiery expressiveness.

Not long after the arrival of Autumn comes Buddy, another rescue. His left eye has a black pirate patch, and there are black spots sprinkled throughout his white coat. He never outgrows his younger brother role even though he weighs nearly three times more than Autumn. He follows his older sister around everywhere, from one bed to the next.

Whenever I take the two of them out for a walk I have to prepare myself for their excitement. Autumn and Buddy are well-trained, but when they are on a leash, they snap into a hypnotic state like Sherlock hounds on a mission. Buddy can easily drag me if I'm not paying attention to the leash.

It drives my brother's allergies crazy to have dog hair everywhere. So when my brother's family moves into their new home, Autumn and Buddy are no longer permitted to sleep upstairs in bed with my niece. However, since my brother often comes home late from work, he's usually unable to enforce the rule.

One night, he comes back from work late and sees Autumn sneaking upstairs, but she can't see him. She stops on the fourth step, certain she heard a noise. Then she continues another few steps before pausing again. *Is the boss home?* She definitely heard something but doesn't see anything. She dashes up the next several steps with the stealth of a feline. This time the boss lets her go without reprimand, for who can blame a canine's heart for wanting to sleep next to her best friend?

***

Molly was my Autumn. I'd sneak her into my room and hide her under the covers so my parents wouldn't catch us nestled together. I am with her when she becomes a mother. Molly struggles to push her last puppy out of her womb. She is weak and tired from having delivered three puppies already. When I find her under my bed, I ask my father why she's hiding in the dark. He tells me that animals go to dark places when they know they are dying. She's been trying to push the last pup out for more than 24 hours. My father takes her to the vet, and I wait at home for him to bring her back. He returns several hours later with a box. In the box, I find the only surviving puppy in the litter. The others did not make it without their mother's warmth and heartbeat.

"Where is Molly?" I ask.

"She's gone to sleep."

The vet had given my father two options: Molly could either have surgery to remove the stillborn puppy or be put to sleep. Seeing the one puppy in the box makes me feel as though my father had not even considered my feelings and how important Molly was to me. The news of Molly brings tears even to my unsentimental mother. Why not pay a few hundred dollars to let my best friend live?

[141]

Thirty years after Molly's passing, Autumn is at the vet clinic after having thrown up all day. The vet tells my sister-in-law that Autumn's heart is bleeding out and that it's only a matter of time before she passes. My sister, who is visiting them, calls to tell me the news. I watch Autumn on video and see her breathing in distress.

"Does *she* know?" I ask my sister.

My sister and I know how heartbreaking this news will be for our niece. The once shy nine-year-old had come out of her shell through her friendship with Autumn. The two were inseparable in their daily routines of sleeping, eating, and school. When my niece went to university, Autumn continued her guardianship of the family, taking care of my nephew, sister-in-law, and Buddy.

"Yeah." My brother is on the way to pick up our niece from the airport. It is only appropriate that my brother is the one picking up my niece to say goodbye to Autumn. The two have a father-daughter bond that I outgrew very early on in my life. Even at age 20, my niece still refers to my brother as "Daddy," and she snuggles next to him while watching TV. I feel both happy and sad when I see the two of them because as my brother's younger sister, I never received much affection from him. Most of my early memories of my brother are of him either sleeping or scolding me for making a mess. He was a real-life version of *Sesame Street's* Oscar the Grouch to me.

My father and brother had a knack for giving unsolicited opinions about my life, even though I never asked either of them for their advice. They mistook my opinions for immaturity, my boundaries for insolence, my voice for childishness. My mother and sisters never discouraged me from pursuing a life in the creative arts, but my father and brother were the two who regularly did so. Over the years, I grew to understand my father's fears. After living through two wars and overcoming extreme poverty, how could he watch his child become a "starving artist"? But my brother, what fears burdened him?

As the only son, primogeniture thrust upon my brother the weight of all the expectations of previous generations. My brother has taken on the dreams of everyone but his own. Not only did he bring home the bacon, but my brother also played soccer-dad so that his wife could fulfill her dreams to become a doctor—even in the absence of appreciation. Though it frustrated the hell out of him, he stayed close to my parents to provide my mother a protective shield from my father.

But, when I hear the news that my brother is picking up his daughter from the airport to say goodbye to Autumn, I am reminded that my brother is more than his father's son or my brother. He is the father of the next generation, and in a single generation, the tides have already turned. When my niece decides to go to art school, my brother supports her unconditionally. She would grow up with the freedom to fully express herself, especially with the ones she loves. It's no easy feat for any man to do that, but if one could, it's my brother.

Auntie loves you, Autumn.

Autumn and Auntie G, 2016

16

UNDERNEATH THE WAVES

I grew up with the influences of dream culture. From kindergarten through high school, I attended Catholic schools where religion class was part of the daily curriculum. The stories that mesmerized me the most were the ones in the book of Genesis; I loved the story of Joseph and his coat of many colors. He was the recipient of great affection from his father, but this attention made his brothers jealous. So, his brothers kidnapped and sold him off as a slave in Egypt. They told their father that Joseph had been killed by animals. Even with this betrayal, Joseph endured with dreams from the divine assuring him that he would be protected. His ability to interpret dreams enabled him to rise through the ranks as one of Pharaoh's advisors and eventually reunite with his family.

In Korea, dreams serve as omens bearing insight into one's future.

[145]

For centuries, dreams were considered so valuable, that they could even be bought and sold. For instance, the *taemong kkum* is a dream about a baby's conception. Family members who see vivid flowers or fruit in their dream know that a baby girl is on the way. If they dreamt of another plant or a vegetable, then a boy has been conceived. When I was conceived, my mother dreamt of two large rooms filled with pink flowers.

A few months before getting married, I had a dream I'll never forget. As I am about to walk down the aisle, dark water begins leaking into the church pews, creating a stench of murky water. Water snakes surround me, and I can't walk down the aisle. My clothes are moist with sweat when I awake. For most, the dream would have an obvious sign that I did not want to get married, but my entire reality was unraveling. I couldn't be sure what was real. The term "gaslighting" had not existed in my vocabulary yet.

Every night I would put my journal on a shelf, and I trusted my ex not to read it. One day, we had a fight about I had written about one of my past relations, and this made him very jealous. He lectured me on the inappropriateness of my thoughts. I told him that I could express whatever I wanted in my journal as I damn well pleased. That led to an explosive fight, and I ended up in the bathroom, crying and hitting my head against the bathroom door.

A few days later, when I looked for my journal and asked my ex about it, he said, "I saw you throw it away." I knew I had not. I kept it in the same spot every day: on the bookshelf. Putting it back on the shelf the last time was what had caused the fight in the first place. I knew I had not thrown it away. But when I told him as much, we got into another fight. He reminded me that I was the irresponsible and ditzy one, so naturally, I had been the one to throw it away. If he had seen me throw my journal in the trash, why didn't he stop me? He knew how important it was to me.

He said he couldn't be blamed for my carelessness. This was not the first time he rewrote events. I started to think that perhaps I was going insane. Ashamed, I locked myself in the bathroom and began cutting myself. This period marked the beginning of self-destructive behaviors.

The dream before my wedding warned me not to walk down the aisle. The snakes showed me what would happen if I got married, but I ignored them. Water symbolizes our unconscious emotions. Snakes are related to healing and transformation in non-Christian cultures, but in Catholicism, snakes represent sin and evil. The marriage was forbidden, and I had failed to recognize the warning.

I also had recurring dreams that would help me understand my conscious emotional landscape when I was unaware of my patterns. In one of them, I couldn't move my mouth or speak because my mouth was full of broken glass. In another, someone was holding me down, and I tried to scream for help but couldn't because my mouth was glued shut.

Others were about climbing buildings. I would climb one building and get to the top, only to see that there was another building to climb. Building after building, I kept climbing. At one point, I stopped to look at what was ahead of me and saw that there was no end in sight

[147]

of buildings to climb. I had this dream throughout my time in business school and during my corporate job.

Most of my recurring dreams stayed the same. There were slight variations, but the endings would be the same, at least to the best of my recollection. As I developed a more consistent meditation practice, I often caught glimpses of my dreams from the previous night, and I could recall them as though replaying a memory. There was a particular one that rolled out like a mini-series drama. Over the years, this series of dreams grew on top of one another; they were all connected.

This series started *in media res* with me alone in the middle of the sea, swimming against the current. Without a lifejacket, I struggled to swim toward shore, but the current kept me in the same place. Exhaustion drowned me. This recurring dream began shortly after I quit consulting, where I was drowning from burnout and suicidal thoughts.

I continued to have the swimming-against-the-current dream over the next several years, as I struggled with much self-doubt about my direction. Some months, life seemed to be going swimmingly well. I'd land a client and begin to feel a bit of momentum, hoping that I was getting into the swing of owning my own business. But after the feast, famine came, and I would berate myself for the lack of clients. *Your work just isn't that great. You're so lazy, and that's why you don't have any clients. You're not doing enough. You're just not good enough to make it.*

The feast and famine cycle caused so much uncertainty, and I couldn't talk to my family about this because they had disapproved of my leaving in the first place. When I wasn't screening my calls and had the strength to pick up my phone, I'd put on a cheerful voice to tell my mother everything was going well. Every call with my father would end with, "Stop wasting your time and money. Come home. I'll buy a business, and you can run it." Thank you, but *NO*.

***

After a few years of re-runs, a new "episode" in this mini-series came out. The last episode would fade out with me sinking underneath the water. The new one began with a close-up of me choking, gasping for air. I'd keep swallowing water, but I was still alive. Something told me to try inhaling instead of gasping. Reason told me there was no way I could breathe, so I'd waffle between calm breathing and bouts of choking. With practice, I discovered how to breathe underwater.

This episode appeared around the fourth year of being an artist. During that time, my confidence as an artist went from belly squirm to a slow crawl. I shared more of my work on Instagram and grew bolder in talking about my work. The Eye See You Project took me around the world, and I found clients more easily. I still had my doubts about calling myself a photographer or artist, but I believed someday would.

Around this time, my relationship with New York began to change. I could no longer see myself living there long-term. Maintaining my mental health in that environment required more effort than I had available. The cost of living required me to prioritize work over self-care. I no longer wanted to be in such a demanding relationship. They say your relationship with New York is like the one you'd have with a toxic girlfriend. "Can't stay, but can't leave." I was getting used to the idea that leaving New York was not a sign of giving up or of weakness, but rather that I was allowing myself to live in an environment that optimized and prioritized my need for less pressure and more space to create.

Several years later, I discovered through astrocartography, that the northeast is not an ideal location for me, and it seemed to make sense. I had never felt quite as at home in the United States as I had when living abroad. Even when I was in unstable political countries like Turkey and Lebanon, I felt a sense of home and security, and that my soul could exhale. Italy had also allowed me so much freedom to live la dolce vita, and I longed for that sense of spaciousness that I could not feel in my 500-square-foot two-bedroom apartment on Prince Street. The fact that I was paying more than a mortgage to live in such an apartment was incredulous. You could get a four-bedroom home with a spacious backyard in Austin, Texas for $2,000, yet I was paying to live on top of people in a place that required cockroach maintenance at $4,100 per month. It's ludicrous to think about how I was able to do all that and maintain sanity. I know friends who lived outside of New York with monthly expenses totaling $3,000.

The struggle, though, was a badge of courage. It was a sign that I was strong—that I was the real deal. Making it in New York meant that I could make it anywhere, right? There may be a bit of truth in this because New York is intense. Life in the big apple requires constant attention and movement, which likely caused my bouts of escapism and release through parties, retail therapy, and candy. The energy of New York is hyper-masculine, which can be altogether exhilarating and exhausting. The constant drive towards somewhere makes deep sleep almost impossible. I wouldn't know deep sleep until I moved to Austin.

***

In the next episode, along came a troubled whale. It needed my help, but I didn't know how I could help. Together we became companions. Over time, I recognized that it was my mother's spirit inside of the whale. She was leading me home.

This sequence of dreams with the whale is a little hazy, so I can't go into specific details other than what I recall feeling. I felt so small next to the whale, yet I didn't feel threatened by her. I sensed that she needed a friend, and I was grateful I was no longer alone, lost at sea.

Animism, the idea that all things living and nonliving have spirits, is in my blood. In Korean culture, before Christianity and Buddhism arrived on the peninsula, there was a very strong tie to animistic practices. Early on in life, I developed a peculiar fascination with animals and my ability to communicate with them. As a little girl, I would play with bees, even at the risk of getting stung, and write stories filled with animal characters. Later I would learn about the concept of animal totems. In the Native American tradition, animals act as guides who bring messages. The spider has been a consistent totem throughout my life, as well as snakes. And when the whale appeared

[151]

in my dream, I immediately woke up and searched for the meaning of whales. They represent the subconscious. The spirit of the whale sings of compassion and is known as Mamacocha or "mother sea" among the coastal tribes of Central America. It is in the belly of the whale where Jonah suffers fire and madness for three days and three nights and prays for deliverance.

For a while, I stopped having dreams about being in the water. I wasn't having as many dreams in general and later discovered there is a correlation between smoking pot and dreaming. I would not remember any of my dreams if I had smoked the night prior. But during the pandemic, I went through a dry spell of no smoking. That's when the dream of being lost at sea came back.

The mini-series would start all over again, beginning with swimming, drowning, and breathing underwater, but then deviating. I'd surface to find myself no longer lost at sea alone. Others were struggling to find their way to shore, but it was the opposite direction that I'd be swimming. I knew the way back, though. I had navigated these seas many times. I knew where to avoid the riptides, and where there were rocks for respite. "Come this way! Trust me!" I'd shout to the others. The next thing I knew, a chain of people was behind me. I swam with one person on my back, and that person had another person on their back, and so forth, and I was guiding everyone back to shore. Even though I knew it would be a while until we made it, I was certain of the direction we were heading.

I know that for many the pandemic was a very scary time, but for me, it was a very exciting time. For the first time, I felt like I knew what I was doing. I had traversed the waters of uncertainty and had been through the most stressful times, uncertain how I would pay my bills. But here I was, still alive and blessed with the opportunity to follow my heart. Even after I was thrown into the deep end, I learned with whale medicine how to move in deep waters.

The pandemic was just the permission I needed to cut loose. I had gotten a call from my client saying they were shutting down, and that was all the confirmation I needed from the universe that leaving New York was the right thing to do. In the previous 72 hours, I had seen the city burrow itself. The subways were practically empty, and as I rode my city bike from the east side to the west side, I could not believe how eerily quiet it was at 7 p.m. The only sign of people included a line wrapped around the corner outside of Trader Joe's, where apocalyptic pandemonium had already begun.

I left New York on Friday the 13th, March 2020, and headed for Austin. It took me a week to fully unwind and decompress from the decision and whirlwind that was happening both externally and internally. But as the storm was growing stronger outside, I could feel a parting of the seas opening inside. I could exhale at last. No one had any answers at the moment, and now I had full permission to make up the rules I had always longed to, without having to swim against a sea of resistance.

As crazy as it sounds, I felt as though my life up to that point was in preparation for the pandemic. For five years, I had been testing unknown waters as a creative entrepreneur. And when the tides changed with the Great Resignation, I surfaced from underneath and began helping others navigate the murky waters of walking away from a job, toward creative pursuits. That's how business coaching and creative mentorship began for me. I decided I would combine the two things I knew and loved best—storytelling and living the stories I wanted to tell. My winding path was finally making sense. Yes, I was swimming through choppy seas, but this time, I was not swimming alone. I was swimming with others.

The day prior, I attended a dharma talk with Drupon Lama Dorje, who discussed the importance of compassion. "You get a small cut on your hand, and the pain is all you can think about until you break your foot, and then you forget all about the pain in your hand." My initial reaction was to resist this analogy. Should we just go around looking at others' misery and comparing our pain to theirs? But then I thought about it another way. When we focus solely on our suffering, we get lost in our misery and feed into the biggest and most harmful lie— that we are alone. The truth is that we are never alone. And that is compassion.

To me, the swimming dream is also about surrendering and letting go. Even when I thought I would drown and die, the ease of the whale showed me how to stop struggling and breathe underwater. There was nothing to fear in letting go.

But it was through all the years of practice in swimming against the current, learning to surrender, and experiencing waves of compassion that I could swim and help others back to shore.

In other words, our struggles bring out our strengths and magic dust. But we don't have to try so hard to swim. Sometimes we can let go and let others show us the way. And with compassion, we can navigate the stormy waters together.

Sunrise, Sian Kaan, Yucatan Peninsula, 2021

17

THE WIND

While living in Tulum, the wind sirened me further into her embrace. I began meditating with her daily, feeling the ebb and flow of her gentle dance across my skin. Instead of staying indoors with the AC on, I spent my summer days at La Pizzine writing outside with 100% humidity at 31° C, happy to play the wind's game of hide and seek. Every time she found me, the wind brought more memories to fill the pages of this book.

In August 2021, we got the warning that Hurricane Grace would be passing through Tulum. The entire town prepared for the wind's spectacular visit, taping glass windows, roping furniture, and sealing leaks. Weeks leading up to the hurricane, I, too, had been preparing for a storm. Thunderous confusion preoccupied my every thought, and I wanted to resolve the turmoil jostling me inside.

Bea, a power *curandera* I had been working with in Tulum, suggested I practice writing with my non-dominant hand to understand my troubles. She told me to buy the book *The Power of Your Other Hand* by art therapist Lucia Capachione. I learned that usage of the non-dominant hand activates the less utilized side of the brain, thereby unlocking the more creative, intuitive, and inner child aspects of ourselves.

One afternoon, as I struggled to focus, I opened my notebook and began writing with my non-dominant hand. I began by inquiring, "What is troubling you?" It was only a matter of time before my hands began auto-scribing a conversation amongst my inner child, authoritative voice, and guides.

Non-dominant Hand: I hate this feeling of trusting and not being in control. I need to know everything is going to be okay. I want it all to be okay. Please tell me it's going to be okay. I'm sick of myself. I'm sick of you chasing and running. Fuck it. I can't stand your imperfection. It's oppressive. All your judging all the fucking time. Go away. Leave me alone. I hate you staring at me. You look at me like I'm so shitty. What did I do to deserve this? You treat me like garbage. What did I do to you? What is it that you're so pissed off about? What are you so angry about? Where did I fuck up? You act as though I was a mistake and never should have been born. I never should have come, is that what you're telling me? Do you want me to die? Do you want me to mutilate myself? *Tell me what you want from me, I'm begging you.* I'm done fighting with you. Please. Please just talk to me. Please just say something to me. You ignore me and the only time you do talk to me is when you're mad at me. Which feels like all the time. You beat me up daily and kick me. I don't want to fight you. I just want to be your friend. Please tell me why you don't want to be friends.

Dominant Hand: I don't know how to be your friend. You let me down. You lead me to places that hurt when I let you do the talking. You get me into trouble. Your stupid dreams are what make my life so difficult. Why can't you just be normal? Why do you have to be so difficult? Why can't you be like everyone else? Why can't you just shut up and behave? You're just creating more pain and misery for us all.

Non-dominant Hand: I'm sorry. I'm so sorry. I'm so sorry you're so hurt. I'm so sorry. How can I help?

Dominant Hand: I don't think you can. You're just too weird and so irresponsible, and you do reckless things. You should be more practical with your finances. You suck at relationships. You can't make up your mind so you keep getting me into trouble. You and your stupid dreams. Nothing can fix the mess you're in. You're reckless and stupid. You don't deserve to talk. Just shut up and give up. You think that life is sunshine and roses when the world fucking sucks. You might as well coast and hide. Stop making so much noise. Shut up. Stop talking. Stop. Just stop. It's pointless. You've fucked up, and now I gotta clean up your mess. When will you ever get it through your head that you're going to fail? You always fail because you're an idealistic fool. You're so naïve and immature. Grow up. That's what you need to do. You're almost 40, and you don't have anything to be proud of. You're a loser, a waste of life. Just stop. Stop trying before you ruin it all. You can't make it because you've never been disciplined. I'm so sick of you fucking up. You're always fucking up. Just give up and get a job. At least you won't be sitting like the lazy-ass you are, pretending to write your book. Give up before you fuck up anymore.

Non-dominant Hand: I'm sorry. I'm just being me, but you keep saying that's unacceptable. I don't know how to be anything else. I don't need you to approve of me, but can you just not yell at me? Please. I don't know what I can do. Please. Please. Please. I beg of you. Please. Why is everything I do wrong?

Dominant Hand: You abandoned me. You quit a steady job, and now I'm stressed out all the time. You said it would be different if you pursued your dreams, but what have you got to show forth? You're a loser. You're such a loser. I want to hit you. I want to shove you. I want to beat you up. Everything about you disgusts me.

Non-dominant Hand: I can't help who I am. Why can't you love me as I am? Please. Please love me. All I've ever wanted was for you to love me.

Non-dominant Hand: *(handwriting changes)* Genevieve—we love you. And that's all that matters. We all love you. You are on the right path. They don't know how to love you because that is not their job. It's *your* job. You loving you. Do you love *you?* You *love* you.

Dominant Hand: Me, love *me?* How am I supposed to love me? How?

Non-dominant Hand: Forget the bank account. Forget your social status. Be outrageously you. Say yes to it all and live on the edge of love.

Dominant Hand: Who is talking now?

Non-dominant Hand: It's us. Your angels.

Dominant Hand: May I know your name?

Non-dominant Hand: Grecia.

With that, my hands stopped, and the trance broke.

***

The eye of Hurricane Grace stood on top of Tulum, waxing from 11 p.m. to 3 a.m. and waning until 6 a.m. That night I stayed awake. Outside my window, I saw trees whipping back and forth, tossed by the wind's wrath. I wanted to go outside and be with the storm, but my better judgment kept me inside. I opted for a compromise and slid my bedroom window open. The howling of the wind flooded my room. As the rain spattered across my face, I made the sign of the cross and closed my eyes.

A familiar scene appeared before me—a whirlpool of energy creating a vortex around a single figure standing in the eye of the storm. It was a scene from Paulo Coelho's *The Alchemist*. I read *The Alchemist* for the first time in high school, and since then it remained a steady companion throughout my life. Santiago, the protagonist, had left the comforts of his home in the Andalusian hills traversing across Northern Africa. There he would meet the wind.

In this scene, though, it was me standing with the wind. As I stood still in the grip of the storm, the wind whispered, *"Watch as I knock down trees and shatter these glass houses. It only takes me a moment. Do you still doubt that I can move mountains for you, my child? You are exactly where you are meant to be. Stay the path. Write your heart out."*

I had been longing to hear this for so long. For so much of my life I had been trying to play catch up with everyone else, never feeling like I was where I was supposed to be—in the wrong career, in the wrong city, the wrong relationship, the wrong weight, and everything else in between. But there, as the wind spoke, I began to relax. *Yes. I am exactly where I am meant to be. I am not here by mistake.*

A prayer flowed out of my mouth: "I am yours. Guide me and I will follow. I want to be guided. Guide me and I will follow. Grant me the ability to hear your voice. May I always hear your voice."

And the wind stopped for a moment with only the drumming of rain on the leaves, and I heard, *"Be still and know that I am God. Be still and know me. Receive."*

I continued repeating aloud, "Guide me, and I will follow. Thank you. Thank you. Thank you. Thank you. Thank you..."

"Receive, dear Genevieve. Write your heart out. Write your heart out. Write your heart out."

When morning arrived, all was silent. No birds. No cars. No electricity. Overnight, the storm washed away all the toxic sargasso that had been lining the beaches. A few days later, the power and water came back, and I resumed kundalini class. The teacher shared, "Our gifts and wounds come from the same place." As he said that, the very same wind that had stormed by a few days ago came back with summer night caresses. ***Yes to it all.***

Little Me, San Diego, California, 1986

Note to Reader

WHERE TO START

During the process of writing this memoir, many shared that they, too, wanted to write a book, but they didn't know where to start. So I wanted to end this book by talking about starting.

I had no idea what I would write when I agreed to write this book. Desiree, whom you know by now, convinced me to start writing one. We lived together during the pandemic, and I watched how excited (and challenged) she was while writing her fourth book. I felt creatively uninspired, hardly touching my camera during the pandemic. "Why don't you start writing a book?" she suggested. But, like all the best advice she's ever given me, it took me months before I warmed up to the idea. Besides not knowing what my book would be about, I didn't think I had the writing chops to do so.

"I'm not even a writer," I told Des. Prior to this memoir, I had written a handful of short stories and articles, and I didn't share much of my work to spare myself the embarrassment. The C that my lit professor had given me for my senior thesis stayed with me: I was a "mediocre" writer at best.

By October 2020, though, I was at my wit's end with no creative outlet and bored as hell from the daily walks in the neighborhood. "Do you really think I can write a book?" I asked Des.

"Yes."

"Okay, I'll do it."

"Really?!"

"Yes, but you have to be my writing coach."

"Done."

Those of you who have no idea what you want to say or are wondering if you have the skills to write a book, know that I was in the same boat as you. But now that I've completed this book, I can confidently say where to begin yours.

The first day I started writing this book, Des and I had just finished eating dinner. She told me to grab a writing notebook. I asked, "Is this our first writing session?"

"Yep," she responds. "If you could talk for days on certain topics, what would those be? Write a list of them."

On the list of 20+ topics, none seemed interesting enough.

"Who's going to want to hear about any of these things?" I whined.

"Just pick *one* of the topics on that list, and write a chapter on that."

"But how do I even know which one to start with if I don't know what my book is about or what direction I'm going in?"

Her response was, "You won't know until you start." That's when was reminded of the anecdote Des had shared with me years ago about Michelangelo's sculpture process.

Michelangelo had inherited a gigantic slab of marble that other artists abandoned, finding the material unusable. That piece of rejected marble turned into one of the world's greatest masterpieces, *David*. Michelangelo said, "The sculpture is already complete within the marble block before I start my work. It is already there, I just have to chisel away the superfluous material."

Before he began chiseling, he started many of his sculptures with sketches and miniature models. From these initial sketches, he began chiseling away, but not without running into roadblocks. He discovered that his measurements had been wrong, forcing him back to the drawing board to recalculate the proportions he initially made. In some areas, he could alter the sculpture with minor adjustments, while in others, he had to scrap it altogether. In essence, he was re-engineering throughout the entire process. Where he started was not where he finished.

With that in mind, I decided to sit my ass down at the computer to start making a few "sketches" for the first chapter. When I started, I felt like I was drinking from a fire hydrant. Ideas spewed out with no hose to direct the flow, nor a filter to parse out the relevant from the crap. But after I let the waters calm, I found a few phrases and scenes I liked and zeroed in on them. I'll fast forward and tell you that by the end of the week, I had one chapter of my book written. Triple fast-forwarding, I ended up chopping this chapter altogether. But taking the week to write this chapter was not a loss. From this first chapter, I discovered other scenes and memories I wanted to explore, some of which ended up in this final draft. The only way I knew what those scenes were was by sitting down to write. Chapter after chapter, I found new breadcrumbs to follow. Nothing is wasted effort in the creative process. It's all part of the journey.

Writing this book was much like driving late at night in the fog. I could barely find my way with the headlights, but it didn't matter. I knew the road would reveal itself as long as I kept driving. Of course, there were detours and dead ends, but nevertheless, I eventually found my way. Over time, I developed my own writing process, and my confidence as a writer grew. It's easier said than done, but after spending my entire life in the creative and business fields, I know that no amount of planning and strategizing will get you to the end of a project until you roll up your sleeves and start.

So where should you start? *ANYWHERE*. As Lao Tzu says, "The journey of a thousand miles begins with a single step." If you have a book in you, follow that desire. It doesn't matter if you know how it's going to end. What matters is that you start. For some of you, it may be in writing to *g@genevievekim.com*. I'll be here to remind you every step of the way that your story matters.

Me at Fazenda Pao Grande, taken by Eduardo Grabowsky, Brazil, 2018

Epilogue

GRATITUDE

O f all the creative projects I have partaken in, writing has been one of the most transformative, particularly, the memoir. I started writing this book with the intention to allow the creative process to guide me throughout the process. I drew on what I learned as a student of many other creative endeavors, including my training in classical music, photography, writing, and yoga. Whether it would just be two people who would read this, my book editor and me, or others came secondary to the learning I'd receive from this project. That is not to say I didn't have my doubts, but I would find a way to re-center myself back to the practice at hand-- focus on the journey, not the destination. Taking on this writing project guaranteed nothing, but the writing spirits told me to keep going even when I got stuck. And I'm so grateful I did.

* TO THE WRITING SPIRITS *

You have been there for me without fail every step of the way, even when I did not seem to always be there myself. Firstly, thank you for gifting me Desiree as my writing coach. She has not only been my best friend in life, but she has been one of the best creative mentors I could have ever asked for. Her wisdom and divine connection to your kind have kept me from running away.

Thank you for bringing me down to Tulum. It was there that I found a way to silence my mind and find the direction to continue writing this book. Tulum was the best place I could have caved myself in as I revisited some of the most painful parts of my life.

Through Tulum's creative feminine energy and community of loved ones, I was able to soften into the process. It is here where you nestled me amongst my Yin sisters and dear Saasilanos. So much gratitude for Janko, Alice, Martin, Sara, Jovana, and Kelly.

Because of Janko and Kelly, I would not have met Bea, who would be one of the most powerful *curanderas* to move through all the shit I was remembering. She introduced me to the book *The Power of the Other Hand*, and from this, I discovered even more of myself.

You provided the perfect den from where I wrote the majority of my book, and I'm so grateful that I could live alongside Elsa, whose inquisitiveness organically drew out memories and times in my life that I had not remembered, and connections I had not thought about.

Even in the dark cenotes, I could hear your encouragement, "We are here. You are not alone." Thank you for ushering in the spirit of the winds to guide me. *Namaste*, Wind, for the prayers you've carried across continents, oceans, and lifetimes.

Delek, dear Spirits, for the soundtrack you blessed me with as I wrote these chapters. Through Milu's set, Santi's trumpet, and Mardeleva's soundscapes. From Christian Loeffler to Max Richter. From the rooftop of Raum Gallery to that of Saasil's. If it weren't for the music of others, I would not have been able to feel the stories.

Spirits, you've been present even before I knew I would write this book. In the sunrise of Oman as I cried alone in the desert. In my divorce papers. In my terrible YouTube scripts. During the moments I couldn't believe I was alive or understand why I was. You were there reminding me at every single step to keep saying yes. You brought me to Pizzine to write nearly every day while in Tulum, amongst friends who would ask me how many words I had left to write. You were there in my writing sprints with my online writing community, The Process.

As Desiree says, writing a book is like playing a game of Jumanji. This was that. The reflections and the Jumanji experiences were an opportunity to rewrite the narrative I had been using against myself. You moved me from titling this book *My Big Fuck Yous* to *Yes to It All*. You helped me forgive and love unconditionally. It's not just saying yes to this and not to that; you taught me how to say yes to it all, and live on the edge of unconditional love with my past so I can fully live now.

Throughout the journey you made it clear where I would go next and you've been laying out the answer to a question I've been banging my head against the wall over for years, asking you for guidance on... Throughout my life, I've worked so hard to find the answers, and in this book, you've shown me how much I've struggled for the sake of struggling as if to say that because I struggled you owed me an explanation. When I got to Tulum you told me, "*Sit your ass down and start writing.*" I got a bit distracted here and there, fearful that if I listened to you I'd somehow end up on the streets or wouldn't be able to support myself any longer.

But when you told me to just finish the damn book, instead of distracting myself with new revenue schemes, I listened. I surrendered. Hell, you even put Michael Singer's book *The Surrender Experiment* in my path several times so that I couldn't help but surrender. With that, in June, July, and August I unwound my need to be a productive businesswoman and focused on being a full-hearted writer, where I rediscovered how to breathe, read, paint, cook, and create without giving into my fears. Though at times I grappled with some Catholic immigrant and Korean guilt about working and suffering hard, you helped me set that goal. Even though I had no clue how I would be able to maintain my lifestyle and pay the bills, you always provided as I wrote.

Today is the eve of my departure from Tulum. You told me a few weeks ago during a meditation, "Your time in Mexico is now complete. It's time to fly again. But first, visit your family because you're going to be in Europe for a while." So tomorrow, I'm driving back to Austin, where I'll get things out of storage before I get back on the road to San Diego, unload head to Portugal.

As I write this, my bags are all packed and waiting for me in my car—the one that only a big brother would generously gift me before I even knew I'd need a chariot for my adventures throughout Mexico.

With me, I'm carrying a heart full of gratitude and love for the family you've blessed me with, for they are my greatest teachers in life. Through them, you showed me how to live fiercely and to love unconditionally. Before you, I lift my hands.

Always your devotee,
Genevieve

* TO THE ONES WHO MADE THIS BOOK POSSIBLE*

Dad, thank you for your courage and tenacity in bringing our family across the Pacific Ocean, worlds away from your own to open a world of new possibilities. Your leap into the unknown is how I came into existence as the first person in our entire family's ancestry to be born outside of Korea. Thank you for teaching me to sing with joy, write every day, get on the road and travel, and photograph memories of a lifetime. You've given me an inheritance worth more than gold—dozens of journals and catalog photos I've filled over the years.

Mom, thank you for your blind faith in me. Even when you could not understand my dreams, you supported them the way you knew best—all while taking care of three other children and making sure the fire in the kitchen remained lit and the family business kept running. Your unwavering devotion to the Mother is now all of ours.

To my sisters, who have both shown me what devotion looks like and have been bright stars in my life. Though you shine so differently, thank you for showing me that faith comes in many shapes. You've each taught me fortitude, faith, and family. To my oldest sister, thank you for teaching me how to pray in the darkness. At 1 a.m. you came to sleep with me and showed me how to pray, even when I had not the strength, and you prayed with me even as a little girl when I was heartbroken. You are my guardian angel in the flesh. And to my other big sister, thank you for showing me what grace, forgiveness, and surrender bring—light even amid such loneliness and darkness and difficulty. Thank you for loving me unconditionally all these years and for encouraging my creative spirit all those Saturdays.

Brother, thank you for caring so damn much about our family and me. Without your sacrifices and love, our family would not be where it is today. I honor the father, son, husband, brother, and most of all man you are.

To the doulas who helped me deliver the words on these pages, I see you. For your hearts and ears throughout the twenty months of gestation, I thank you. Through my ghosting, moaning, and scavenging, I love you. The women in A Creative Mastermind, especially Sam—for Thursdays. Sara—for your irreverence. Elsa—for the sanctuary. Kelly—for Peter Pan and cacao balls in silence. Bea—for the wisdom of the other hand. Jen—for the title and taps. Komal—for the simplicity. Yin Sisters, especially Magdalena—for reminding me to dance. Esther—for the word counts. Aster—for the unconditional

[174]

Cristina—for kundalini. Kimi—for being such a 10. Alice—for singing with vibrato. Matisse—for getting pony-stoned. Apollonia—for weaving dreams. The women of P.S. Circle—for your courage. Andrea—for kilometers on the road. The women of The Beauty That Surrounds You, especially Sahar, Chandani, Virani, and Sonia—for teaching me how to pray. Andrea—for your generosity. Henley—for your words. Lex—for your story and holding mine. Madeleine— for your acute understanding of language. Desiree—for without you the chapters in this book would not exist.

To the firekeepers, I see you. Ziad—for seeing the hakauati in me before I could. Jeff—for opening your heart to the world. Janko—for chilcuague on the scooter on the way to Darwin's late-night tacos on the playa. Prakesh—for the mudras. The Process, especially Paul—for the timer. Dushan—for no expectations. Justin—for the rose quartz. Jesse—for the safari in Austin. Jacob—for gorilla glue. The men of La Pizzine, especially Roberto and Luis—for the space to write and drink lattes. Samarth—for your trust. Eduardo—for Marchador Life and showing me Grandfather. Axel—for your birthday. James—for finding the eccentric. Diego—for building a bridge from Mexico to Costa Rica closer. Andreas—for being my partner, co-pilot, and apprentice; we are unconditionally one. David—thank you for holding me accountable and sharing the magic of constellations. Tigre—for sharing your home. Tyohar—for silence. Milu—for your soundtrack. Santi—for your tenderness. Jonathan—for being Human. Rodrigo—for seeing me. Nayef—for opening your doors, LA to Lisboa. Perry— for 7Flowers and the garden view.

[175]

To all the artists who helped me finish this book, mostly to Christian Loeffler and Nihls Fram, whom I listened to for hours on end. You were the soundtracks to feeling this work to its completion.

* TO THE EARTH THAT GROUNDED ME *

Austin, thanks for bringing me back to life with your deer and water snake. If you were ever wondering what East meets West would look like, well, just look out and you'll see it's neither Southeast nor Southwest, it's the South all in her lonesome star. But from there I could travel to Knoxville and back and then back to Las Cruces. What a rainbow that you should bring me to birth my book alongside my partner in crime, yoni steam sidekicks, whiskey and hookah nights, between YouTube recordings and wiping up Ayla's pee while making Isaiah a snack before going to Ninja Warriors while Aiden is learning how to be the man of the household. To Nature's Treasures and cleanses. Hallelujah, thank you for the creative residency, Austin!

Tulum. Oh, Tulum. There could be a whole book on you alone. From La Veleta to Uh-may, from the cenotes to Sian Ka'an, from Ikal to Milum, I adore listening to the soundtrack while driving on my scooter. From cave diving in pitch-black darkness to dancing with the family at RestAura. From cartel to construction, we will do our part to protect you. From Buddhist chanting to Mayan fires. We all gather from the winds of the South, West, North, and East. You cast the prayers and voices into Yemanja, who remembered to reflect Luna y

Sol across her hair.

San Diego, for keeping my family healthy, nourished, and alive. You gave me a reason to celebrate. My mother's 80th birthday. A once-in-a-lifetime opportunity to say thank you, Grandmother and Grandfather, for bringing her forth. Hallelujah, we've all made it here together. God damn.

Costa Rica, you brought me back to the land that called my sister and her family to live a life that today I have seen unfold before my very eyes. A land where we come back to silence, in awe of birds, spiders, mosquitos, and monkeys. Barefoot we come back home to the silence of listening meditation, and mystery in the maloka. From altars, we see a spark across the fire to bring us from darkness to light underneath our grandfather's sky, fire and peyote. Our ancestors see us and call us to lift each other, from Malpais to Pachamama, from one wave to the next jungle party. All the elements lining up with enough wood to burn the fire next to the dirt roads between the ocean. From father to mother, brother to sister, I see myself in each of you. And in your reflection, I sing *hey hey hey ho.*

In the rolling hills of mágico Mexico, as I entered your portal through the Laredo Border, I opened my eyes to see the frontier. Real de Catorce, you showed me from what a sacred place Grandfather came. Then down to your sirens in San Augustin, then east to Bacalar and Palenque, and to the north San Miguel de Allende and Mexico City, Todos Santos, Ziahuatanejo, San Luis Potosí, Oaxaca, Merida, Valladolid, Monterrey, Valle de Bravo. Mexico, you have always been my neighbor, ever since I was born on the other side of the border. I'm glad I got to understand the true meaning of es tu casa.

Back again to San Diego, the land from which I came, of the Kumey-aay (Cuyamaca Rd) that dwelled in the Baja California greater circle. You are the seed from which it all began, and now I'm riding back to you with stories in pursuit of the call.

Here, in Lisbon, I complete this book. Thank you to the land that already feels like home.

And to those of you who are still reading, *you got this.* **You got this.** *I got you.* **I got you.** *We got this.* ***We got this.***

Wherever we go next, may our ancestors keep calling us. Thank you to my two grandmothers, and the mothers of my grandmothers.

Gracias a la vida.

Silence, Tulum, Mexico, 2021

About the Author

Genevieve Kim is a storytelling polymath at the intersection of creative direction, business strategy, travel, economics, performance art, the natural world, media, and spirituality. She known for using her unique perspective to provide a loud physical manifestation to human courage, vulnerability and dignity as preserved through her lens. She is a world-hungry savant whose multifarious life experiences in opera, photography, digital media, design and writing, have enriched her creative approach with a high-octane curiosity towards each of her projects.

Here life's work is to help others tell their stories and to celebrate life's work is to help others tell their stories and to celebrate the unique and universal across the human experience. In addition to working as the creative director and founder of media production studio *Triangleflash.com*, Genevieve also gives live performances, creative workshops, and retreats. She is currently based in Lisbon, Portugal You can visit *GenevieveKim.com* to learn more.

Reading a book written by a friend has helped me realize just how little we know about the people around us and what they have experienced in life. Its opened another level of empathy in my heart for not just the faceless "numbers" but people directly around me.

Its clear that ∅ is an artist and she lives her life like its an artwork that defies definition. In a world that thrives on branding and narrative, she has been thoroughly undefinable.

Made in United States
North Haven, CT
20 September 2022